brickwork & paving

for house and garden

brickwork &paving

for house and garden

Michael Hammett

The Crowood Press

First published in 2003 by
The Crowood Press Ltd
Ramsbury, Marlborough
Wiltshire SN8 2HR

www.crowood.com

British Library Cataloguing-in-Publication Data
A catalogue record for this book is available from the British Library.

ISBN 1 86126 602 2

Illustration credits
All drawings are by Claire Upsdale. The assistance of the Brick Development
Association is acknowledged in their preparation.

The author is grateful to the following companies and individuals for the
supply of and permission to reproduce photographs as follows. Baggeridge Brick
plc: pages 6, 101,102, and 111; Belle Group: pages 37, 38, and 118; Bovingdon
Brickworks Ltd: page 23; Brick Development Association: pages 32, 54, 72, 79
(bottom), 80, 110, 113,114, 115,121 and 122; British Cement Association: page
36; Building Cosmetic Services: page 143; Sue Duncan: page 7; Freshfield Lane
Brickworks Limited: page 18; Hanson Brick Europe: page 12; Kingscourt Brick:
page 48; Caroline York: page 8; and The York Handmade Brick Co Ltd: pages 21
and 123.

All other photographs are by the author who also acknowledges The National
Trust for kind permission to reproduce the picture of Tattershall Castle (page 10)
and to Mr Christopher Parker for kind permission to reproduce the picture of
Faulkbourne Hall (page 11).

Typeset by Jean Cussons Typesetting, Diss, Norfolk

Printed and bound in Malaysia by Times Offset (M) Sdn Bhd

Contents

CHAPTER 1

Introduction

Brick is an important building material in many parts of the world. In Britain, brickwork masonry has become a particularly well-established, well-developed and versatile form of construction. Because of its attractive appearance and superior properties of robustness, durability and low maintenance, it is the most popular material for building the external walls of houses. Brick is also appropriate for garden landscape features, especially when used in conjunction with clay pavers.

The successful application of brick depends on a basic appreciation of the variety of products included under the general description 'brick' and also on the nature of brickwork and how detail design affects appearance. This book provides informative comment on these matters, guidance on specification and basic information on the techniques used in simple brickwork for house and garden construction.

Over 90 per cent of bricks used in Britain are clay bricks. Bricks are also made of concrete – crushed rock aggregate bound with Portland cement. Sand, lime and crushed flint are used to make calcium silicate bricks, which are also known as sandlime and flintlime bricks. In some countries, bricks made from these alternative materials have a greater share of the overall market than they do in Britain.

Pavers are made of clay, but concrete pavers have the lion's share of this market as they cost less to produce. The information and comments in this book are primarily concerned with clay bricks and clay pavers, but many of the comments and descriptions of work apply to all material types. Manufacturers' recommendations should be followed on matters of detail specification.

Bricks are an ideal material in the domestic environment.

Garden walls and paving.

SCOPE OF THIS BOOK

The aim of this book is to provide information and guidance for general readers who are attracted to brick and would like some help in understanding the nature of bricks and mortar. It deals with the proper specification and construction of brickwork and brick paving in houses and gardens. Some detailed description of the tools and procedures involved in bricklaying and paving are included, which should help DIY enthusiasts expand their technical appreciation of brickwork, but the book is not primarily an instruction manual for craftsmanship training. It should assist readers to specify work and check that it is being built correctly by employed builders.

TECHNICAL CODES AND STANDARDS

Readers do not need to be knowledgeable about the details of building construction. Technical jargon and formalized technical specification have been avoided. The use of some technical terms has been considered desirable and their definitions are given in the Glossary at the end of the book.

In describing some materials, reference to British Standard Specifications has been unavoidable because they are the descriptions used by building materials suppliers.

At the time of writing, some of the relevant British Standards (BSs) relating to materials are in the process of being withdrawn and replaced by European Standards (ENs), others are about to be similarly superseded. All ENs related to matters quoted in this book are expected to be adopted prior to its publication. Nevertheless, because there will be a period of about two years during which reference may be made to either BS or EN terminology, both references are included in this book. This will also allow comparison with other guidance that may not include reference to the EN terminology.

METRIC AND IMPERIAL DIMENSIONS

Since the 1970s, the construction industry in the UK has been using the metric system exclusively for dimensions, weight and volume. However, many people outside the industry are more familiar with imperial measurements and have little 'feel' for metric dimensions. Because this book is for general readers, both metric dimensions and their imperial equivalents are given for general descriptions and some details of construction. For materials and their specification only the metric system is used to avoid the possibility of confusion and inaccuracy.

BUILDING REGULATIONS AND PLANNING CONTROL

Brickwork may be applied to many projects associated with houses and gardens. Some will be of a scale and type that, in the UK, might require official sanction in connection with the Town and Country Planning Acts and Building Regulations. Some projects that are quite large do not require planning permission because they fall within the category of permitted development. Rules for this are subject to change and if projected work affects the exterior of a building, particularly at the front, it is sensible to make an informal check with the Local Authority Planning Department.

Special conditions apply to work on buildings within Conservation Areas and to buildings that are 'listed' as being of special historic or architectural importance. The Local Authority Planning Department will be able to offer advice on these matters too.

Independent of planning controls, work on buildings must be in accordance with Building Regulations. The Local Authority Building Inspector will advise if a formal application for Building Regulations Approval is needed.

Boundary walls and fences require Planning Permission if they exceed a height of 1m (3ft 3in) adjacent to any public highway or right of way, or 2m (6ft 6in) on boundaries with other properties.

Garden structures are not subject to Building Regulations but, for safety reasons, it is very important that freestanding and earth-retaining walls are properly designed and built. Chapter 4 refers to authoritative published guidance, which will be appropriate in many cases, alternatively seek the assistance of a structural engineer.

BRIEF HISTORICAL BACKGROUND

Brick is man's oldest manufactured building material. In world terms it is over ten thousand years old. The ancient civilizations in Mesopotamia and Egypt were prolific users of sun-dried clay (adobe) bricks for their buildings, not only for modest dwellings but also for their huge ziggurats and pyramids. They also fired clay bricks to make them stronger and more durable for use in the construction of river walls and hydraulic works. The Bible records that the Tower of Babel was built of burnt clay bricks, as were the walls of the city of Babylon. Both adobe and fired bricks were used in the world's oldest town, Jericho, dating from the tenth millennium BC. Inexpensive, vermin-proof, fireproof, and with excellent insulating properties, adobe bricks are still used today in regions with a dry climate. Countless millions are used in Africa, the Middle East, Asia and Central and South America.

In making fired clay bricks, the burning process transforms the natural clay into an inert, semi-vitrified material that will no longer revert to a mud-like state when soaked in water. Fired bricks are more durable than sun-dried ones and, therefore, more versatile in service.

The Romans first introduced brickmaking and brick masonry to Britain. Brick was a principal building material in the Roman Empire and their Legions set up brick and tile factories throughout their colonies. Although Roman buildings were often faced with elegant stone or marble, or with finely finished sand and lime plaster, the structure was frequently of brick masonry. Alternatively the structure was of stone rubble with brick used for bonding courses to provide stability and for the more regularized parts of the construction like quoins and the surrounds and arches to window and door openings.

The Roman Legions withdrew from Britain in AD412 and subsequently all but a very few of their buildings fell into ruin. Interestingly, their bricks have survived long after their buildings and they can be seen reused, centuries later, in Anglo-Saxon and Norman buildings.

Making sun-dried bricks in Nigeria.

Roman bricks in house at Herculanium.

Burgh Castle, Norfolk – bricks as bonding courses in Roman fortified walls.

St Albans Cathedral, Hertfordshire – reused Roman bricks.

Holy Trinity Church, Colchester – reused Roman bricks.

For example, in Colchester, Essex, the Church of the Holy Trinity has an Anglo-Saxon tower of rough stone with a large quantity of reused Roman bricks to bond them. The quoins and door and window openings are formed exclusively from Roman bricks. In Hertfordshire, the bricks in the transepts and crossing tower of St Albans Cathedral were taken from the ruins of the nearby Roman town of Verulamium and used by Norman builders in the twelfth century – nearly a thousand years after they were made and first used.

Roman bricks are of different sizes and proportions to medieval and modern ones. They are large, generally square and thin.

A Roman brick, Ephesus.

Following the fall of the Roman Empire, brick-making disappeared in most of Europe. In the medieval period, it spread slowly north again from Italy and Byzantium, where the technology had been kept alive. Regions where good building stone was scarce were generally rich in clay deposits and therefore the reintroduction of brickmaking was very expedient. Strong trading links between northern Europe and the eastern counties of England saw the technology reintroduced into Britain in the thirteenth and fourteenth centuries.

These medieval bricks are of very different proportions to the Roman ones. They are small, oblong

Tattershall Castle, Lincolnshire.

blocks, easy to lift in one hand and, with a trowel of mortar in the other, lay to form brickwork. They are sized so that they bond together, overlapping regularly, without having to be cut to fit – so their size and proportions are eminently practical.

Immeasurable quantities of bricks like these were used over the next centuries but, initially in England, the new brick was a very prestigious material. It was also expensive and its early use is seen in grand houses, medieval castle-like buildings, built by the rich and influential of the mid-fifteenth century. Tattershall Castle in Lincolnshire, Herstmonceaux Castle in Sussex and Faulkbourne Hall in Essex are excellent examples.

At first bricks were handmade by itinerant brickmakers, generally setting up brickmaking on the building site to produce bricks for that building only. But brick was quickly accepted as an attractive, durable and versatile building material. It passed from being a select material for the privileged few, to become a staple of British building, and as such it was to grow in popularity over the next centuries.

Until about 1800, all bricks were handmade; not only was the clay placed in moulds by hand, but all the other activities of making involved manpower.

Faulkbourne Hall, Essex.

Handmaking a brick.

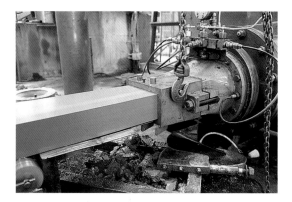

An extrusion machine.

Digging the raw material, barrowing it from the clay pit, preparing and mixing it with water for moulding, setting bricks in and drawing them from kilns were all done by hand, because no suitable machinery existed. In the nineteenth century two significant changes to brickmaking occurred simultaneously – the development of machinery and the discovery of new raw materials.

With the general development of industrialization in the nineteenth century, mechanization was applied to brickmaking. Machinery was introduced for preparing the clay and for forming bricks by moulding, pressing and extrusion. Improvements in kiln design and later the development of continuously burning multi-chamber and tunnel kilns, increased efficiency as did the use of coal, coke breeze and oil as fuels.

Prior to this period, only the shallow lying deposits of alluvial clays and brick earths were accessible for brickmaking, but in the nineteenth century mining for coal and other minerals led to the discovery of different types of clay. Dense shales and fireclays, found in association with coal measures and rock-like marls, proved to be excellent raw materials for brick. They required heavy machinery to pulverize, grind and mix them into a plastic consistency for forming into bricks.

A multi-chamber Hoffman kiln.

Typical Victorian terraced-housing in North London.

A modern house in North Oxford.

The nineteenth century saw the expansion of brickmaking into a highly developed industrial activity, stimulated by a huge demand for its products by the burgeoning economy of Victorian Britain. Popular demand for bricks and development of brick production processes continued throughout the twentieth century and into the twenty-first.

It is significant that no single production technique has been adopted to the exclusion of alternatives. The diversity of clay materials used, and the different techniques for forming bricks and firing them, give rise to differences in appearance and physical properties that are admired and desired. To maintain great variety, many of the techniques associated with early brickmaking, and its intermediate development, still persist within the modern industry. Today Britain is unique in having an industry that manufactures an exceptionally varied range of clay bricks.

TRADITIONAL BRITISH REGIONAL CHARACTERISTICS

In pre-nineteenth century Britain, before the development of canals and railways, road transport was dependent on the horse and cart, and haulage of heavy goods was expensive. As a result, when new building work required large quantities of bricks, and suitable clay was available, brickworks were

Modern bricks are produced in great variety of types.

frequently set up alongside to make the bricks. This procedure was continued throughout the nineteenth century for some of the huge civil engineering structures such as the tunnels, retaining walls, bridges, viaducts and similar structures associated with the canal and railway systems.

Permanent brickworks were established to supply building needs, but bricks tended to be used within a limited area around the site of their production. Records show that, typically, the cost of bricks doubled if delivery distance increased from five miles to ten.

The characteristic appearance of older brick buildings often varies from region to region because of the colour, texture and physical properties of the different bricks available in each location. For example, the gault clays of Cambridgeshire gave rise to the prevalence of creamy, buff coloured bricks to be seen in the brickwork in that part of England. In contrast, the

hard-edged, precise, smooth appearance of brickwork in the north of England is built of smooth, dense engineering bricks. These are made from local carboniferous shale clays by machine pressing or extrusion and wire-cutting. A deep red colour is typical, but restricting oxygen in the kiln (reduction firing) produces the blue colour that is characteristic of some of engineering bricks, e.g. Staffordshire blues.

Different again are the red bricks characteristic of south-east England. They are made from the iron oxide bearing weald-clay of Sussex and Kent. Traditionally they have been produced by handmaking, or by simple machine moulding, and have a rugged texture and a comparatively high water absorption. Variations in firing that occur in simple kilns and clamps, particularly when wood fired as was once common, give the multi-coloured appearance of southern counties stock bricks. Brickwork built with them tends to have a warm, rustic character.

Georgian London stock bricks in Clerkenwell.

As already noted, the building of the canal system in the early nineteenth century and the railway system later, were major users of brick. When in operation they became the providers of economic transport of bricks to the communities they served. For example, London's St Pancras Station Hotel was built of bricks from Nottingham brought by the new railway. Similarly, the Liverpool Street Station complex was built with bricks from Lowestoft. There was a substantial and constant demand for bricks in London and countless millions of them were brought into the capital by railway, canal and river transport. The horse and cart, however, was still required for the transfer from railhead or quayside to building site, and this was not to change until the widespread introduction of steam traction engines and then petrol and diesel powered heavy lorries in the twentieth century.

London was unusual in being served from so far afield, but it did present an exceptional demand. The

Gault bricks in nineteenth-century almshouses, Cambridge.

fletton brickmakers in the Northamptonshire and Bedford regarded London as there primary market. With works nearly ninety miles north of the metropolis they were quick to exploit cheap transport by rail. There was local brickmaking too, and in 1939 there were 367 brickworks in the Home Counties serving the Greater London area.

By the end of the nineteenth century brick was the staple building material in the British Isles, and towns in all but the most sparsely populated regions were served by brickworks. Up until the outbreak of the Second World War in 1939, the majority of bricks were used within thirty miles of where they were made.

The Second World War necessitated the closure of hundreds of brickworks and, with the return of peace, town and country planning controls and economic considerations precluded the re-establishment of a great number of them. The industry never re-established the very high volume of production that characterized the latter half of the 1930s. There was a substantial demand for building materials to meet extensive repair and redevelopment programmes in the following decades, but brick and brick masonry were strongly challenged by 'new' materials and construction systems like concrete blocks, asbestos cement and metal sheeting, plywood, wood particle boards, glass and reinforced concrete and steel framed structures. Nevertheless, brick remained an important and popular material in British building and a directory of clay industries published in 1962 lists nearly 700 brick manufacturers, some having several individual works.

In the final decades of the twentieth century many brickworks closed, and amalgamation and acquisition of some of the old companies also occurred. By

Staffordshire blue bricks in village school buildings, Warwickshire.

the end of the century the number of brick manufacturers has reduced considerably. A fall in demand for bricks because of reduced building programmes, economic recessions and changes in construction were obvious contributory factors, but planning restraints on clay extraction, demands of environmental legislation and escalating fuel costs were also important influences. Production capacity is still very high and variety very diverse, but a more rationalized brickmaking industry has emerged into the present century. The number of brick manufacturers in the British Isles is now less than one hundred. Many use one type of clay and one manufacturing technique, but there are a few very large organizations with

Sussex stock bricks in new house.

several brickworks, so their product ranges include bricks made from a variety different clays and by different processes.

Although regional characteristics are apparent in the brickwork of many older buildings in Britain, the localized pattern of use, already eroded to some extent by the railway and canal transport, was profoundly changed by dramatic developments in road transport in the latter half of the twentieth century. Improvements in roads and the development of a comprehensive motorway network, coupled with the development of large capacity lorries equipped with self-unloading devices allow manufacturers to deliver bricks direct to a building site within hours.

For aesthetic reasons, new building is frequently required to use materials that match or are similar in character to locally existing ones. Even when there is no need to match, inevitably there will be personal preference of particular types of bricks. The brick industry is still able to provide its customers with an exceptional choice of bricks and clay pavers.

CHAPTER 2

Brickwork Materials

BRICKS – VARIETY AND APPEARANCE

There is a very wide choice of clay bricks available. Manufacturing methods have developed over hundreds of years and today sections of the industry are highly mechanized and efficient. Nevertheless, some manufacturers still continue to use traditional methods in order to maintain certain favoured characteristics of their products. Clay is no longer dug by hand, forked-over and trod underfoot with water to work it into a mouldable state; such artless labour can be done much more effectively by machine. However, some bricks are still made by hand, one at a time in individual moulds, and some are fired in primitive clamps rather than in modern, computer-controlled, fuel-efficient kilns. The use of such traditional methods persists because they give unique texture and coloration to the products.

In contrast, other bricks are made very efficiently in huge quantities by highly developed, modern, machine methods and continuous firing kilns. These too have appearance characteristics derived from particularities of their production and the different types of clay used.

Because of differences of production and raw materials each brick product is unique. Some differences are obvious, others quite subtle. Between 1,200 and 1,500 different bricks are currently available in the British Isles. A range unequalled anywhere else in the world.

Depending on the type of clay, bricks are fired at temperatures between about 900°C and 1,200°C. Colours of clay bricks are generated by the reaction of the constituent minerals to the intense heat of firing.

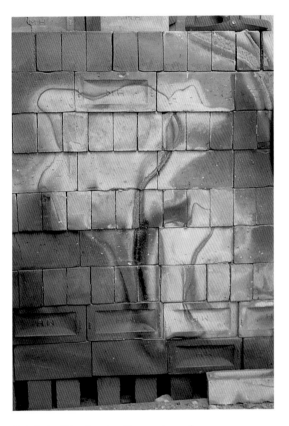

Bricks in kiln showing fire marks and coloration.

The yellow, pink, orange, purple and black colours in the photograph above, are the result of variations in the firing 'climate'. The clay is consistent, but minor differences in temperature and oxygen supply at the surfaces of each brick has affected the

Blue and red engineering bricks.

coloration – sometimes quite dramatically. As the bricks are taken out of the kiln they are sorted by colour into several groups that are marketed as different varieties.

BASIC TERMINOLOGY

As might be expected from a technology hundreds of years old there are many terms to describe different types of bricks. Some are described in the Glossary. Others, although they once had specific meanings, have become obsolescent and have no formal standing in the context of modern building. Technical terms that are used in contemporary building specification and standards relate to significant aspects of quality, performance and usage, therefore it is important to understand their meaning.

Facing Bricks (or Facings)

Bricks of a consistent colour and texture, reasonably free from surface damage or blemishes, intended for building brickwork of consistent and attractive appearance. Most bricks on the market are facing bricks.

Handmade stock bricks – the curved crease marks should always 'smile' (not 'frown').

Common Bricks (or Commons)

Bricks without any guarantee of consistent surface appearance. They are intended for use in brickwork where consistent colour and texture is not of primary importance, e.g. backing walls, internal brickwork, foundations and brickwork that will be covered with cladding or some other applied finish.

Engineering Bricks (or Engineers)

Clay bricks that are particularly strong and dense, and conform to specific standard tests to measure their compressive strength and water absorption. Historically their primary use was in civil engineering construction, e.g. bridges, tunnels, quays and earth-retaining walls, but other types of bricks are sometimes used for such works. Similarly, engineering bricks are not limited to civil engineering work and are used for many types of building.

They are typically a strong red or a dark blue colour and smooth in texture. They are often specified for face work but, unless the manufacturer confirms otherwise, do not assume that an engineering brick will have the consistent appearance expected of a facing brick.

Stock Bricks (or Stocks)

This term was originally used to describe handmade bricks formed in a frame mould located on a workbench by a wooden 'stock', which forms the bottom of the mould. Such bricks are made with clay of soft mud consistency containing a proportion of ground fuel material to aid firing. Traditionally they would be fired in a 'clamp'. Although such bricks are still produced, the term has now been extended to include machine and handmade bricks made from soft mud clays, not necessarily with fuel added or fired in clamps.

Handmade bricks usually have curved crease marks on the surface and this is a characteristic feature. Black spots are also common on multi-coloured varieties; these are derived from particles of fuel added to the clay during its preparation to aid thorough burning of the brick during the firing process.

Stock bricks are typically, although not exclusively, of high water absorption and of low or modest compressive strength. They often have excellent frost resistance.

The term 'stock brick' should not be confused with references made by merchants or brickyard staff to bricks that they have available, i.e. 'in stock'.

Fletton Bricks

These are pressed clay bricks made from a unique clay that occurs in the East Midlands of England. It was originally found in the village of Fletton, near Peterborough, in 1881. It contains sufficient fuel to fire the bricks and consequently allows exceptional economy in production and very competitive pricing. Rail and road transport was a well-developed part of its marketing strategy and the fletton became an exceptionally popular brick type throughout Britain, especially for house construction and industrial building. Originally flettons were made as common bricks, but facing varieties were introduced in the 1920s by applying textures and sand to the surface of the bricks prior to firing. Fletton facing bricks are now available in a range of colours and textures.

Wirecut Bricks

These are a very familiar form of machine-made brick. Clay of stiff consistency is extruded through a rectangular steel die to form a length of clay with a width and thickness equivalent to the length and

Facing bricks – extruded wirecut and fletton bricks.

width of a brick. The strip is then cut into individual bricks by taut wires spaced equivalent to the height of a brick. To control the flow of the clay, rods are located in the throat of the extrusion machine, these produce perforations in the bricks. Straight from the extruder the clay has a smooth surface, but it may be textured in some way, e.g. with combs, cutters or rollers fitted to the exit from the die, or sand may be applied to give a granular texture.

Multi Bricks (or Multi-Coloured)

A descriptive term meaning that the coloration of the brick varies across its surface and is not exactly replicated on every brick in a batch. Such bricks are intended to be laid randomly to produce an overall consistently blended appearance.

RECLAIMED BRICKS

Brickwork often develops an attractive appearance as a result of years of weathering and this attracts some people to the use of reclaimed bricks. There is a ready market for them, but they are less widely available and more expensive than new bricks. Reclaimed bricks may be justified on aesthetic grounds, but they must be technically appropriate for the work proposed, and frost resistance is a very important consideration.

Many dealers supply reclaimed bricks graded by quality of appearance, but they cannot always guarantee durability. Before the early part of the twentieth century, bricks would have been sorted on the basis of durability by both manufacturers and by bricklayers who would have selected those appropriate for the face of walls exposed to weather and relegated less frost resistant ones for use in the protected inner walls of buildings. During demolition great care must be taken not to mix internal quality bricks with the more durable external ones. To assume that because a brick is old, it must be of proven frost resistance is quite wrong. Furthermore there are no British Standard tests for reclaimed bricks and those for new ones are not applicable.

Unless there is assurance regarding the durability of a particular consignment of reclaimed bricks, they should be only be used where construction details provide protection from severe exposure, i.e. treat

Multi-coloured stock bricks.

them as Moderately Frost Resistant category bricks as described on page 27.

For paving, bricks must be eminently frost resistant. Reclaimed pavers can be used with confidence, but caution is advised if reclaimed walling bricks are being considered for use as paving.

The high cost of reclaimed bricks is a reflection of demand and the cost of reclamation, rather than their intrinsic quality. Considerable labour is involved in demolition, cleaning off old mortar, selecting, stockpiling and handling. The cost of using reclaimed bricks is also increased because a greater allowance will be required for wastage due to selection.

If reclaimed bricks are to be used, make sure that there is a sufficient quantity for the whole of the work, as it is likely to be difficult to find matching ones from another source.

Simulated Reclaimed Bricks

Reclaimed bricks often have a distressed appearance (chips, scuff marks and staining) as a result of service, weathering and the process of reclamation. This can give an attractive, rugged character to brickwork built with them. To emulate these characteristics, some brick manufacturers tumble new bricks and perhaps apply 'attractive' disfigurements, such as random paint marks, whitewash. Simulated reclaimed bricks have the great advantage of being made to conform to British Standards for new bricks with regard to technical properties. They are readily available, are repeatable and are very competitively priced.

Specially Matched Bricks

When existing buildings, particularly old ones, are extended, altered or repaired it might be felt necessary to seek reclaimed bricks to match. It is interesting to note that when brickwork is repaired in important historic buildings, such as Hampton Court and Kew Palace, new bricks are normally specified, albeit made to the particular sizes and special shapes required.

New clay bricks are available in a very wide range of colours, textures, sizes and shapes, enabling a good match to be found for most existing brickwork. There is a large price range, but new bricks invariably cost less than reclaimed ones.

BRICK SIZES

The dimensions of bricks are not arbitrary. A brick is sized so that it can be lifted and manipulated with one hand. Its width and height are related to its length, so that when several are laid to build brickwork, they bond together by overlapping regularly, without having to be cut to fit.

Obviously the dimensions of proposed brickwork should be compatible with the modular system of brick dimensions. Some slight adjustment is possible by reducing or increasing the width of the mortar joints, but for good appearance the width of joints should be consistent throughout the work and so it is always best to use 'brick dimensions' for brickwork.

Today the vast majority of UK bricks are made to a British Standard size, so that architects and builders can design and build brickwork knowing that bricks

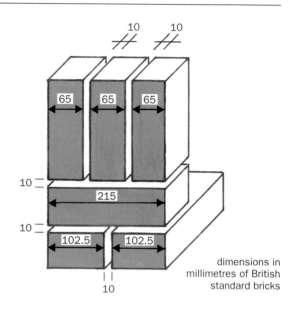

Diagram showing the relationship of brick dimensions.

can be used easily, irrespective of which company has made them. This is very convenient and is a great advantage in the general course of building.

Standardization was initiated by the Royal Institute of British Architects and the Brickmakers Association in 1904 and later adopted in the British Standards Institution specifications.

Originally the dimensions were in Imperial measure (inches and fractions of inches). The construction industry changed to metric measure in the 1970s and the dimensions of the standard brick were very slightly reduced. The modern metric standard brick is 215 × 102.5 × 65mm. With an allowance of 10mm added to each dimension for mortar joints, this gives a co-ordinating size of 225 × 112.5 × 75mm. Four courses of bricks and mortar measure 300mm high; this is very slightly less than 12in, which was the measure of four courses of Imperial-sized bricks. Four standard bricks and joints in a row measure 900mm; again this is slightly less than the 36in that four Imperial-sized bricks would measure.

It is perhaps appropriate to point out that when it adopted the metric dimensional system, the British construction industry decided to use metres and millimetres. Up to 10m, dimensions are generally stated in millimetres, e.g. 2400mm rather than 2.4m. The sizes of masonry materials and components are therefore quoted in millimetres. Centimetres are not used.

In the early 1970s, to promote rationalization in building construction, metric modular bricks with sizes based on increments of 100mm were introduced. There were two sizes: 290 × 90 × 90mm and 190 × 90 × 90mm; with the addition of 10mm for mortar joints the co-ordinating sizes were 300 × 100 × 100mm and 200 × 100 × 100mm. Three courses of these measured 300mm high. Versions with a height of 65mm instead of 90mm were also made. Four

Special thin bricks – 41mm high and 248mm long – give this brickwork a very refined appearance.

Metric modular bricks – 90mm high and 190mm long – give these bricks a chunky appearance.

courses of these measured 300mm high, which conformed to the characteristic scale of conventional brickwork and for that reason they were preferred by many architects.

Metric modular bricks enjoyed some support, particularly for work undertaken by public authorities, e.g. housing, health, education and police buildings, but they never became very popular. In the main this was for aesthetic reasons, although they were also more expensive than bricks of normal standard size.

Bricks are also made of sizes other than those of standard metric or metric modular dimensions. Thinner varieties produce an attractive, refined character to brickwork and have always been popular, e.g. 50mm high bricks that (with 10mm joints) rise five courses to 300mm. They are sometimes referred to as Tudor bricks, as they are very similar in size to English bricks of the fifteenth and sixteenth centuries.

In the northern counties of England and in Scotland many bricks used in the nineteenth and early twentieth century tended to be larger than those used elsewhere. Four courses and joints frequently measured 13in high (330mm), sometimes 14in (360mm). Many manufacturers in the north of England and Scotland make these large bricks today in order to enable repair work and new building to match.

Such large bricks are inevitably more expensive than normal ones, and to provide a more economic alternative, some manufacturers also make bricks that conform to metric standard bricks in length and width, but match the thickness of the larger traditional types. These are used in extension work that co-ordinates with other modern components on plan, but allow matching of the coursing of the original brickwork. Although the new brickwork does not exactly match the original it is more in keeping with its character than would be the case if the altogether smaller metric standard brick was used.

BRICKS OF SPECIAL SHAPE

Normal format bricks can be used to build most brickwork, even quite decorative and intricate forms, but brickmakers also produce accessory bricks of various shapes and sizes that are referred to as 'specials'. These are used to turn corners other than at a right angle, form curved work, arches, chamfered edges, splayed plinths, sills, cappings and copings. Some of these forms can be built by cutting normal bricks and piecing them together in the work, but this can be very complicated and requires considerable skill to obtain a satisfactory appearance. Using specials provides a neater, simpler and more robust construction.

A bay window built using internal and external angles and plinth special shapes.

An extensive range of standard specials for use with metric standard bricks is specified in British Standard BS 4729: *Dimensions of Bricks of Special Shapes and Sizes*. Brickmakers supply most of them to order, but some of the more popular shapes are available from stock. Some brickmakers also make additional specials to supplement or extend the standard range. Where justified by the importance of the work, or the quantity required, purpose-designed special-shaped bricks can be made to order for a particular application. Such bespoke bricks are referred to by brickmakers as 'special specials'. They can be expensive, especially if only a few are required.

A selection of special-shaped bricks.

TECHNICAL CONSIDERATIONS

Most bricks are chosen primarily for their appearance, and in many instances any brick will be satisfactory from a technical standpoint. However, there are applications that require particular technical attributes and the suitability of a proposed brick must be decided by checking on its physical properties as declared by its manufacturer in trade literature.

In the UK and Ireland, clay bricks are manufactured to conform to the British Standard BS 3921: *Specification for Clay Bricks*. At the time of writing, the draft European Standard for clay bricks is awaiting approval by the member states of the European Union. When it is approved, it will be introduced as BS EN 771-1: *Specification for Clay Masonry Units* and the BS 3921 will be withdrawn, although for a couple of years both standards will be available as alternative specifications. Both standards deal with measurement and classification of the physical properties of bricks with reference to their effective technical performance in service. Manufacturers routinely provide the following information on their products:

- resistance to damage by frost action;
- soluble salts content;
- compressive strength;
- water absorption.

Frost-damaged bricks in the top of a boundary wall.

Resistance to Damage by Frost Action

Knowledge of a brick's resistance to damage by frost action is essential when choosing a suitable brick for use in the external walls of buildings or in external works, e.g. boundary walls. For such works the standards define three categories of frost resistance, as shown in the table below.

In practice, moderately frost-resistant bricks (M or F1) can be used for the external walls of many buildings. Such walls are vertical and most of the rain

Frost-resistant categories in British and European standards for bricks			
Performance	**BS 3921 category**	**EN 771-1 category**	**Description of suitability**
Not frost resistant	O	F0	Bricks suitable for internal use but if used externally are liable to be damaged by frost action if not protected by impermeable cladding.
Moderately frost resistant	M	F1	Bricks durable except when in a saturated condition and subjected to repeated freezing and thawing.
Frost resistant	F	F2	Bricks durable in all building situations, including those where they are in a saturated condition and subjected to repeated freezing and thawing.

driven onto the wall surface by wind will be rapidly shed. Wetting will normally be restricted to a few millimetres near the outer surface of the wall. Saturation is extremely rare, provided that the top of the wall and the wall areas below window openings are protected by roof overhangs, projecting weathered copings and window sills. Flush-finished cappings and sills do not provide adequate protection. Moderately frost resistant bricks are not suitable for the construction of copings and window sills themselves. A recessed joint profile should not be used with moderately frost resistant bricks as they impede rainwater run-off and encourage wetting.

Frost-resistant bricks (F or F2) can be used wherever moderately frost-resistant bricks (M or F1) are suitable, but must be used if a design includes brickwork subject to saturation. The degree of exposure to wetting is difficult to predict but, as common sense will confirm, water stands on flat surfaces and will not run off sloping surfaces as easily as it will from vertical ones. Brickwork forming such surfaces, e.g. brick-on-edge cappings, copings, sills and paving, together with brickwork immediately below that receives water running off them, is likely to become very wet and often saturated. In this state, freezing will cause ice to form within the brickwork and there is the danger of permanent damage if the materials are not frost resistant.

A proposed construction should be considered to assess the exposure that the various parts of the structure will be subjected to. A brick should then be chosen on the basis of it being capable of withstanding the 'worst case' exposure. It is impractical and undesirable to specify different bricks for the various parts of a structure on the grounds of varying frost-resistance requirements. A particular brick product will have a frost resistance derived from the clay and the firing process, it will not be available in alternative categories of durability to suit different applications.

A manufacturer's declaration of frost resistance is reliable, i.e. moderately frost resistant (M or F1) and frost resistant (F or F2). No physical characteristic is indicative of frost resistance. In particular, the belief that the strength and/or water absorption of a clay brick gives an indication of its frost resistance is incorrect.

Incidentally, bricks of category O or FO 'not frost resistant' are not made by British manufacturers.

Soluble Salts Content

The clays from which bricks are made sometimes contain soluble salts, which might still remain in the brick after firing. Fuels burned during firing may also add some salts. In small quantities these salts are harmless to properly fired bricks, but soluble sulfates can damage cement mortar.

Bricks are tested for soluble salt content in accordance with the standards. Content is limited by defined maximum percentages, by mass, of soluble salts. Two categories are defined in BS 3921: low (L) and normal (N); and three in EN 771-1: no requirement (S0), a normal level (S1) and a low content (S2).

In practice, soluble salt content is significant when deciding what mortar to use for brickwork. When bricks with normal levels of soluble salt content (categories N and S1) are to be used for brickwork that is liable to be substantially wet for prolonged periods, the mortar must be resistant to damage by sulfates (*see* page 31 for mortar durability). In bricks with low soluble salt content (categories L and S2), the quantities are considered insufficient to constitute a risk to the mortar.

In BS 3921, frost resistance and soluble salt content of bricks for external use are combined and expressed as a durability designation: FL, FN, ML or MN.

Sulfate attack of mortar joints.

Compressive Strength

Clay bricks are load-bearing materials and come in a various strengths from about 7 to over $200N/mm^2$. In order to design economically, structural engineers need to know the particular strengths of the bricks and mortars they use so that they can calculate brickwork strength. Therefore, bricks are tested and manufacturers declare their compressive strength. Clay bricks of $50N/mm^2$ or greater strength may be classified as 'engineering bricks', if they also have low water absorption.

The strength of any clay brick will not invalidate its use for brickwork in buildings of domestic or similar scale or in garden works. The load-bearing requirements of such applications are modest enough to be satisfied by bricks of the lowest strength obtainable, and bricks cannot be too strong.

Water Absorption

Some bricks are very porous and can absorb a lot of water, others are very dense and can hardly absorb any. A standard test procedure measures water absorption by weighing a dry brick, boiling it in water for five hours, to drive out air and encourage maximum water absorption, and then weighing it again. The increase in weight is expressed as a percentage of the weight of the dry brick. Water absorption (WA) varies from less than 3 per cent to over 30 per cent. In general, water absorption should not restrict the choice of bricks, but it can be significant in three contexts:

- *The definition of 'engineering bricks'.* BS3921 defines minimum strengths and maximum water absorption for class A and B engineering bricks. Traditionally, high strength and dense fabric are considered to be particularly appropriate for civil engineering applications.
- *The definition of DPC bricks.* A brick with a low water absorption reduces the amount of water that may rise by a 'wicking' effect, up into brickwork from the ground. Low water absorption bricks built in two courses or more, with lapped joints and dense mortar, act as a damp-proof course (DPC) to resist upward movement of water in brickwork. Two categories of DPC brick are specified in BS3921: category 1 (max. 4.5 per cent WA) may be used in the construction of buildings, landscape and civil engineering work (free-standing and earth-containing walls); category 2 (max. 7 per cent WA) may be used in landscape and civil engineering work.

Two courses of DPC bricks at the base of a free-standing wall, resist rising damp.

- *Rain penetration.* For brickwork where resistance to penetration by wind-driven rain is important, low water absorption bricks are sometimes considered an advantage. However, because these bricks will only absorb a small quantity of water, most of it will run down the surface and into the joints. An alternative theory favours high water absorption bricks because they mop up some of the rainwater and reduce the quantity reaching the mortar joints that, as experience shows, are the route by which the majority of water penetrates any brick wall.

Although there are these differences in behaviour, other factors have much greater influence on resisting rain penetration, e.g. solid filling of mortar joints, wall thickness, cavity construction, DPCs, cavity trays, and so no favour is given to bricks with either high or low water absorption.

MORTAR FOR BRICKLAYING

Mortar is used as a jointing material for masonry. It is also used as a surface-coating material, when it is referred to as a render coat, or rendering.

The colour and texture of sand varies from source to source and has a dominant effect on the appearance of mortar made with it. Colour differences can also be apparent in lime and Portland cement from different suppliers. They also affect the colour of

The effect of coloured mortar – the bricks are the same throughout, the joints were 'pointed' with three different mortars.

the mortar. When matching existing brickwork, matching the mortar is as important as matching the bricks. Even when matching is not necessary, choice is preferable to leaving its appearance to chance.

It is obvious that mortar is an essential component of brickwork, nevertheless its technicalities are often misunderstood and scant attention is paid to its proper specification and use. As a consequence of a lackadaisical approach, failure of mortar is not infrequent and casual advice is often incorrect.

The principal constituent of mortar is sand, the particles of which are bound together, and to bricks or blocks, by a binder. Sand has voids that even its finest particles are unable to fill completely. A well-graded sand will have the least amount of void, nevertheless it will be about one-third of the total volume. This proportion of void to solid dictates the volume of the binder in a mortar because it should just fill the voids. Therefore a normal mortar is comprised of three volumes of sand and one volume of binder. Historically, until the early twentieth century, the binder was normally hydraulic lime. In modern mortars, Portland cement provides the adhesive function of the binder and other materials are added to control strength and improve workability.

Hydraulic lime mortars are still used in the repair of old brick and stone masonry and Chapter 6 contains further information. For new work, Portland cement mortars are more straightforward and versatile.

Portland Cement Mortar

'The mortar should never be stronger than the bricks' is a well-known maxim. In this context, 'stronger' does not relate to load-bearing capacity, but to hardness and permeability. The advice discourages brickwork in which porous, open-textured bricks are surrounded by hard, dense mortar joints. In such brickwork, rainwater wets the bricks, but the impervious nature of the mortar stops the water diffusing and drying out freely. Ideally brickwork should have a similar porosity throughout its mass.

Portland cement is a strong bonding material. Mortar made of 1:3 Portland cement and sand is very strong and durable, but it is also dense, hard and brittle. These characteristics make it unsatisfactory for general use.

The dense, hard and brittle characteristics of 1:3 cement and sand mortar can be reduced by reducing the cement content and substituting filler material to preserve the 1:3 ratio of binder to sand. Lime in the form of dry hydrated lime powder is a beneficial filler as it has good water retentive properties, which promote bonding and improve workability. This type of mix, known as cement:lime:sand mortar, also has the long-term beneficial property of self-healing in the event of minor cracking. This gives the brickwork a tolerance of minor masonry movement.

Alternatively, compensation for a reduction of cement volume in the binder can be made by creating minute bubbles of air in the mortar. This is done by adding an air-entraining agent (plasticizer) to the mortar, in powder or liquid form, prior to mixing. In this type of mortar, known as plasticized cement:sand mortar, dosage of plasticizer and mixing times are prescribed to produce the controlled quantities of air appropriate to the various mixes. Machine mixing is essential. This type of mortar is not suitable for mixing by hand.

Reducing the cement content of the mortar reduces its durability, but air entrainment in the mix improves resistance to both frost action and sulfate attack. 'General purpose mortars', a modern development of Portland cement:sand mortar mixes, combine the advantages of lime and air entrainment in the binder.

The table below lists four types of mortar based on Portland cement as a binder and the proportions, by volume, of the constituents in various mixes. The mixes are grouped in four designations of approximately equal strength and durability.

Mortar Durability

There are two aspects of durability relevant to mortar: resistance to frost action and resistance to sulfate attack.

Mortar in a saturated or near-saturated state, and subjected to alternating freezing and thawing, is at risk of frost damage that would cause it to crumble apart.

The presence of soluble salts in clay bricks has already been explained. In brickwork that is wet for

Mortar mixes (proportions of materials by volume)				
Type of mortar	**Cement:lime: sand**	**Masonry cement: sand**		**Cement: sand (plasticized)**
Binder content	Portland cement and lime, with or without air entraining additive	Masonry cement containing Portland cement and lime in approx. 1:1 ratio, and air-entraining additive	Masonry cement containing Portland cement (min. 75 per cent) and inorganic materials other than lime and air-entraining additive	Portland cement and an air-entraining additive
Designation (i)	1:0 to ¼:3	–	–	–
(ii)	1:½:4 to 4½	1:3	1:2½ to 3½	1:3 to 4
(iii)	1:1:5 to 6	1:3½ to 4	1:4 to 5	1:5 to 6
(iv)	1:2:8 to 9	1:4½	1:5½ to 6½	1:7 to 8

Note 1: The range of sand volumes noted in this table allow for the differences in grading on the void volume. The lower volumes apply to type G graded sands of BS 1199 and 1200, and the higher volumes to type S. Mortar with both lime and air entrainment can be used with any sands within grading defined in BS 1199 and 1200.

Note 2: Mortar mixes that may be recommended for repair of historic brickwork may differ from those in this table.

Sulfate attack of brickwork joints in the top of a free-standing wall.

long periods, soluble sulfates in the bricks can be dissolved and moved in solution to the mortar joints, where chemical reaction with a constituent of Portland cement may occur and cause disintegration of the mortar.

Mortar with a high Portland cement content (i.e. 1:3 cement:sand) is strong and durable. Reducing cement content, as already noted, generally reduces strength and durability, but inclusion of both lime and air entrainment in a mortar binder provides resistance to damage by frost and soluble sulfate reaction, as well as improving workability during laying.

Structural engineers use the compressive strength of mortars when calculating the strength of brickwork, but in buildings of domestic or similar scale, and in garden works, brickwork is rarely highly stressed and so compressive strength is not normally important. Durability, however, is very important for all external brickwork. The table on page 33 lists various brickwork structures giving specification details for clay bricks and mortar.

Materials for Mortar

Sand

Sand for mortar should be 'well graded', which means that there should be an even distribution of particle sizes from the coarsest to the finest, without excess or omission of any particular particle size. It is preferable that the particles are angular and sharp edged, rather than rounded and polished. Sands for mortars are often referred to as 'builder's sand', 'bricklayer's sand' or 'mortar sand', and ideally they should conform to BS 1199 and 1200: *Specifications for Building Sands from Natural Sources.*

'Soft sand' should not be used for mortar as it contains fine silt and clay particles that can lead to shrinkage. 'Sharp sand' is also unsuitable because the lack of fine particles causes poor water retention making it harsh and unmanageable to use.

Sand is sold by weight and measured in tonnes. Small quantities are available in bags. Sand should be stored in clean conditions to avoid contamination and should be covered to prevent excessive wetting or drying out.

Portland Cement (PC) – Formerly Known as Ordinary Portland Cement (OPC)

This is the cement normally used as the binder constituent providing adhesive function. It must be kept dry prior to use. It should conform to BS 12, class 42.5/32.5 (BS EN 197) and is supplied in 25kg bags by various manufacturers, e.g. in the UK, Castle, Blue Circle, Rugby and Buxton Lime. Standard and premium grades are made, the latter having additives to enhance ease of spreading and water retention in mortars and improve long-term frost resistance.

White Portland cement is available for use with white sand and aggregates to make white mortars and white concrete. These materials are expensive. When white mortar joints are required, build the brickwork in ordinary mortar and use white mortar to complete the joints by pointing.

Sulfate-Resisting Portland Cement (SRPC)

A variation of Portland cement in which the material that might react with soluble sulfates to cause damage to the mortar is minimal. It should conform to BS 4027, class 42.5 and is supplied by various manufacturers. It must be kept dry prior to use.

Masonry Cement

A pre-mixed blend of Portland cement (approximately 75 per cent), an inert filler material and an air entrainer (plasticizer). The filler can either be hydrated lime or finely ground rock material. They should conform to BS 5224 and must be kept dry prior to use.

Specification for clay bricks and mortar used in various building situations

Situation	Brick durability BS 3921	EN 771–1	Mortar designation	Remarks
1.0 Work below or near external ground level				
1.1 Low risk of saturation with or without freezing	FL, FN, ML or MN	F1 or F2: S0, S1 or S2	(i), (ii) or (iii)	
1.2 High risk of saturation, with freezing	FL FN	F2: S2 F2: S1	(i) or (ii) (i) or (ii) with SRPC	
1.3 Drainage manholes	FL, FN, ML or MN	F1 or F2: S1 or S2	(i)	
2.0 External walls of buildings (unrendered) excluding chimneys, parapets, cappings, copings and sills				
2.1 Low risk of saturation	FL, FN, ML or MN	F1 or F2: S0, S1 or S2	(i), (ii) or (iii)	
2.2 High risk of saturation	FL FN	F2: S2 F2: S1	(i) or (ii) (i) or (i) with SRPC	
3.0 Parapet walls (unrendered)				
3.1 Low risk of saturation, e.g. low parapets with copings on some single storey buildings	FL or ML FL or MN	F1, F2: S2 F1, F2: S1	(i), (ii) or (iii) (i), (ii) with SRPC or (iii) with SRPC	
3.2 High risk of saturation, e.g. where only a capping is provided	FL FN	F2: S2 F2: S1	(i) or (ii) (i) or (ii) with SRPC	
4.0 Cappings, copings and sills				
4.1 Cappings, copings and sills	FL or FN	F2: S1 or S2	(i)	Bed DPCs under cappings, copings and skills in the same mortar
5.0 Free-standing garden walls				
5.1 With coping	FL or ML FN or MN	F1, F2: S2 F1, F2: S1	(i), (ii) or (iii) (i) or (ii)	(ii) mortar with SRPC in exposed locations
5.2 With capping	FL FN	F2: S2 F2: S1	(i) or (ii) (i) or (ii) with SRPC	
6.0 Earth-retaining walls (backfilling with free draining material is strongly recommended)				
6.1 With coping and waterproof membrane on retaining face	FL or ML FN or MN	F1, F2: S2 F1, F2: S1	(i) or (ii) (i) or (ii) with SRPC	
6.2 With capping, or with coping but no waterproof membrane on retaining face	Fl or FN	F2: S1 or S2	(i)	A waterproof membrane on the retaining face is strongly recommended
7.0 Rendered external brickwork • Single leaf walls and parapet should only be rendered on one face • Parapets and chimneys require copings				
7.1 External walls, chimneys and parapets	FL or ML FN or MN	F2 or F1, S2 F2 or F1, S1	(i), (ii) or (iii) (i) or (ii) with SRPC	When FN, MN or S1 bricks are used, mortar for base coat of render should be made with SRPC

Masonry cement simplifies making mortar on site. It is a complete binder and only requires mixing with specific proportions of sand and water to form mortars to suit different masonry materials. Manufacturers supply masonry cement in 25kg bags under various proprietary names, e.g. in the UK, Brickbond, Limebond and Mastercrete. Some are made with SRPC to give greater protection against sulfate damage.

Hydrated Lime

This is lime in a fine powder form that is supplied in 25kg bags and should conform to BS 890 (BS EN 459). It has no appreciable setting and hardening properties. It should be stored dry. If it gets damp it may go lumpy, but it will not be harmed by this, although it will make mixing more difficult.

Mortar colour matches brick colour to enhance contrast (see also page 20).

Mortar Plasticizer

Air entrainment (tiny bubbles) in a mortar can improve its workability – the ease with which it can be handled and spread with a trowel – and reduce the need for water to keep the mortar fluid during laying. In the long term, air entrainment also benefits mortar durability, improving resistance to frost action and sulfate damage. The percentage of air entrainment must be carefully controlled, because excess air is detrimental to durability and adhesion. Manufacturers of mortar plasticizers provide instructions regarding dosage and mixing times to generate the required air entrainment.

Plasticizers may be in powder or liquid form and should conform to BS 4887:Pt 1. Domestic detergents (e.g. washing-up liquids) are not acceptable substitutes for mortar plasticizers. They are not made for use in mortar and their foaming action cannot be suitably controlled. The often-heard 'trick of the trade' about adding washing-up liquid to the mortar to make it more manageable is very poor advice and should never be followed.

Anti-Freeze Additives

Anti-freeze additives are not recommended for use in brickwork mortars, even though they are known to be satisfactory in concrete. Those that work by raising the temperature in the material by accelerating the cement setting reaction are not effective with such thin layers of mortar. In addition, some contain chemicals that have detrimental effects on brickwork.

Colouring Pigments

As already noted, mortar colour depends on the colour of the sand, the lime and the cement. It can also be coloured by the addition of pigments that are available in powder form. They are 'earth colours' (reds, browns, buffs, yellows, greys and black) and are inert mineral materials, typically metallic oxides, conforming to BS EN 12878. They do not stain or dye the mortar, the pigment particles are held in the mortar matrix. Pigments were used to make the different coloured mortars used to point the joints in the brickwork work shown in the photographs on this page and page 30.

Small amounts are very effective, but pigment should not be added to mortar in a quantity greater

Lime/sand ready-mix for mortar.

that 10 per cent of the cement, by weight; 3 per cent is the limit for carbon black because of its extremely fine particles.

It is difficult to maintain colour consistency if pigments are added to mortar mixed in small batches. It is preferable to mix together all the sand, lime and pigment needed for a job and use it as described below for 'ready mix'.

Converting Weight to Volume

Sand, cement and lime are measured by volume for mixing as mortar, but they are sold by weight.

The density of sand varies according to geological origin, particle size and shape, and moisture content. A typical density of 1,670kg/m³ is used when estimating quantities. When sold by weight it is measured in tonnes; 1 tonne (1,000kg) is approximately 0.6m³. Small quantities are available in bags.

Cement and hydrated lime are sold in bags of 25kg. Based on a density of 1,400kg/m³ the volume of Portland cement in a 25kg bag is 0.0178m³ (17.8ltr). Lime is a much lighter material, a density of 560kg/m³ is typical and a 25kg bag contains 0.0446m³ (44.6ltr). These figures can be used to assess the quantity of cement and lime required for mortar.

The binder materials (cement and lime) in a mortar occupy the space between the particles of the sand. Their presence does not increase the volume of the mortar and, therefore, the required volume of cement and lime can be calculated directly from the ratio of mortar constituents, e.g. to make 1m³ of a 1:1:6 cement:lime:sand mortar will require 0.166m³ of cement (0.166/0.0178 = 9.36 bags) of cement and 0.166m³ of lime (0.166/0.0446 = 3.73 bags) to be mixed with 1m³ of sand (1.67 tonnes).

Ready-Mixed Mortars

Lime/Sand 'Ready Mix'

Appropriately proportioned quantities of lime and sand, mixed together in bulk, can be delivered to site by specialist suppliers. For use, measured quantities of 'ready mix' and Portland cement must be mixed together with water to make a complete mortar.

Normal deliveries are in 10-tonne batches (4.6m³) in drop-end skips, but for small jobs some companies will deliver 2 tonnes (approx. 1m³). Some supply 'ready mix' in large polypropylene bags. Colour pigments can be included and normally a plasticizer is incorporated to effect air entrainment when the mortar is mixed. If the quantity required is sufficient to justify its use lime/sand 'ready mix' is very convenient, it promotes good consistency of colour and simplifies mixing on site.

The mixture should be slightly damp, 'earth dry'; it will then keep well. Store in clean conditions, prevent contamination and cover to prevent excessive wetting or drying out. Failure to protect can be the cause of colour inconsistency because fine particles of lime and pigments can be washed away by rain or blown away by wind.

Retarded 'Ready To Use' Mortars

Fully made-up mortars are supplied, ready for use, in bins or tubs by specialist mortar manufacturers. These mortars include a chemical additive that delays setting for periods from up to seventy-two hours. When the mortar is laid, the reduction of its moisture content, caused by water being drawn from it by absorption of the bricks, cancels the retarding action and the mortar sets normally. When not in use, the mortar must be kept in the covered watertight container in which it is supplied. If the mortar is not used up within its specified working life, it must be discarded. Typically manufacturers supply retarded 'ready to use' mortars in 0.25m³ covered containers, in theory enough to lay 600–800 bricks.

This form of mortar normally includes air entrainment, and colour pigments can be included. It is very convenient, but may not be economical if the size of the job or rate of bricklaying is insufficient use the mortar within its working life.

BS 4721 covers the specification of ready-mixed building mortars, including lime/sand 'ready mix' and retarded 'ready-to-use' mortars.

Dry Pre-Packed Cementitious Mortar Mixes

For small jobs and minor repairs, dry pre-packed mortar mixes conforming to BS 5838:Pt 2 are available in two types. A general purpose mix for laying brick and blocks and pointing is available in 25kg bags and a higher strength, more durable mix for use where there is exposure to severe wetting and frost is available in 25kg, 10kg and 5kg bags. These mortars only require the addition of water and mixing before use. Restricted shelf-life and expense make them uneconomic for extensive use, but they are convenient if only a small quantity of mortar is required.

Mixing Mortar

The materials for mortar are measured by volume. Any clean container can be used to measure each material consistently. A bucket is convenient for small quantities. A larger bin can be used if it can be tipped out easily when full. Measuring by shovelfuls is not accurate enough.

Retarded ready-to-use mortar delivered to site in sealed bins.

A regular-size tilt-drum mixer.

Mix only enough mortar that can be used within two hours. After two hours it will begin to set and must be discarded. Within this period, if workability of the mortar is reduced because of loss of water by evaporation, clean water can be added to restore its condition.

Mortar should be mixed by machine, except where only small quantities of mortar not containing air-entraining plasticizer are required. A tilting drum concrete mixer is recommended. Small capacity (85ltr) electric or petrol powered machines are available for use where heavy duty diesel powered building site machines would be too large. Both types are available from tool hire companies.

When mixing by machine, load about three-quarters of the sand, or ready mixed lime:sand, and some water. While mixing, gradually add any lime, plasticizer and the cement, and continue mixing. Load the remainder of the sand, or lime:sand mix, and complete mixing, adding water to obtain the required consistency. Alternatively, add half the water and all of the cement and mix. Add the lime and sand and any plasticizer. Continue mixing, adding water as required.

In general, a mixing time of three to five minutes after all ingredients have been added will be sufficient to get uniform consistency. When plasticizers are used, prolonged mixing will cause excessive air entrainment, which will be detrimental to mortar strength, adhesion and durability.

A mini tilt-drum mixer.

Mixing by hand should be done with a spade or shovel on a clean watertight surface. A sheet of 6mm thick plywood approximately $1.2m^2$ is convenient. Mix all the dry ingredients together until the colour is consistent. Add and thoroughly mix in about three-quarters of the water. Add water to get the correct consistency.

ESTIMATING QUANTITIES OF BRICKS AND MORTAR

As a rough guide, a two-storey detached house with a total floor area of $200m^2$ ($2,000ft^2$) and with external walls predominantly brick-faced, will require about 14,000 bricks. With prices varying from about £200 to £550 per thousand, the cost of bricks would be between £2,800 and £7,700. Compared with the total building cost (excluding design and finance expenses), the cost of bricks is unlikely to exceed 6 per cent – probably less than the kitchen fittings that may well be renewed in a couple of decades; the bricks never will. About 70 per cent of the exterior of the building will be brick and so care in making the right choice is very important.

When the dimensions of the brickwork to be built are decided, the quantities of materials required can be calculated. Do not overlook the brickwork below ground level. The height of the walling is from the top of the foundation concrete to the top of the brickwork behind the roof eaves (normally the height of the top of the timber wall plate to which the roof timbers are fixed).

To assess the area of brickwork, it is convenient to calculate the total area of external wall surface and deduct from it the areas of window and door openings and any wall finish other than brickwork. The area of the triangle of a gable wall, i.e. the area below the verge of a pitched roof, is half the width of the triangle multiplied by its height.

For a normal cavity wall with an outer leaf of brickwork and an inner leaf of blockwork, the brickwork outer leaf is 102.5mm thick.

It is usual to order concrete blocks by quoting surface area of walling in square metres rather than the number of blocks. Of course blocks will probably be required for walls within the building as well. A block (215mm high × 440mm wide) is equal in surface area to six bricks. The mortar required for 100mm thick blockwork will be 36.5 per cent of that calculated for an equivalent surface area of brickwork (using the figure in the table below for 102.5mm perforated wirecut bricks).

The quantities of bricks and mortar in the two tables below have been calculated assuming the use of standard bricks with a work size of 215 × 102.5 × 65mm and mortar joints 10mm wide.

For mortar, three figures are given for each wall thickness, depending on the form of the bricks being

Quantity of bricks and mortar per square metre of wall surface				
Wall thickness (mm)	Number of bricks	Mortar (m^3)		
		Perforated wirecut bricks	Shallow frogged bricks or deep frogged bricks (laid frog down)	Deep frogged bricks (laid frog up)
102.5mm	59.26	0.019	0.023	0.030
215mm	118.52	0.047	0.055	0.068
327.5mm	177.78	0.082	0.088	0.107
440mm	237.04	0.106	0.120	0.146

Quantity of mortar per 1,000 bricks			
Wall thickness (mm)	Mortar (m^3)		
	Perforated wirecut bricks	Shallow frogged bricks or deep frogged bricks (laid frog down)	Deep frogged bricks (laid frog up)
102.5mm	0.32	0.39	0.50
215mm	0.40	0.47	0.58
327.5mm	0.43	0.49	0.60
440mm	0.44	0.51	0.62

used and, in the case of bricks with a deep frog, how they are laid:

- perforated wirecut bricks – it is not intended that mortar should fill the perforations;
- bricks with a shallow frog (about 5 per cent of the gross volume of the brick) laid frog up and bricks with a deep frog laid frog down;
- bricks with a deep frog, laid frog up – a frog of 10-20 per cent of the gross volume of the brick is assumed, e.g. a pressed fletton brick.

Allowance for Handling and Wastage

The quantities of bricks and mortar given in the tables are calculated. Bear in mind that bricks are supplied and handled in bulk, normally in packs of 450–500, and that transportation and mechanical handling inevitably cause chipping and other minor damage to a small number of bricks. Within the construction industry it is common to allow an additional 5 per cent for handling and wastage when calculating brick quantities and 10 per cent when calculating the quantity of mortar.

Special-Shaped Bricks

When placing orders for bricks, include details of any special-shaped bricks required for sills, arches and non-right angled corners, as these may have to be made to order. Special-shaped units are more expensive than standard bricks and are supplied in the numbers required. It is wise to order a few extra to allow for errors in measurement or accidents.

A Worked Example

Estimating the bricks, mortar and cement required to build a free-standing wall 215mm thick, 12m long and 1.8m high from the top of the foundation to the underside of the coping units. Perforated wirecut bricks are to be used and 1:½ : 4½ cement:lime:sand mortar.

Surface area of the brickwork:	12m × 1.8m	= 21.6m^2
Number of perforated wirecut bricks for 215mm thickness	21.6 × 118.52	= 2560
	5 per cent wastage allowance	= 128
	Total	= 2688
Volume of mortar		
• calculated on surface area of wall (m^2):	21.6 × 0.047	= 1.015
	10 per cent wastage allowance	= 0.102
	Total	= 1.117m^3
• calculated on quantity per 1,000 bricks:	2.560 × 0.4	= 1.024
	10 per cent wastage allowance	= 0.102
	Total	= 1.126m^3
Mortar constituens:		
Sand (typical density 1670kg/m^3)	1.126 × 1670	= 1880kg (1.88 tonnes)
Cement (in 25kg/0.0178m^3 bags)	Volume 1.126/4.5	= 0.2502m^3
	0.2502/0.0178	= 14.06 bags
Lime (in 25kg/0.0446m^3 bags)	Volume 1.126/4.5/2	= 0.1251m^3
	0.1251/0.0446	= 2.8 × 25kg bags

Summary: *Say 2,700 bricks*
                 2 tonnes sand
                 14 × 25kg bags of cement
                 3 × 25kg bags of hydrated lime

WHERE TO BUY MASONRY MATERIALS

Bricks and Pavers

Brick manufacturers make a range of bricks and pavers. The extent of individual company ranges will depend on their size and the variety of their manufacturing facilities and raw materials. All manufacturers will have illustrated information of their products and many have websites with details. Several will supply customers direct and some have special services for self-build customers. Others that have limited sales facilities will refer customers to selected agents, brick factors or builders merchants to deal with orders and arrange delivery.

Contact details of manufacturers can be obtained from manufacturers' trade associations. The Brick Development Association represents the majority of manufacturers in the UK and Ireland and similar organizations in some other countries are noted in Useful Contacts at the end of this book.

Brick factors are dealers who specialize in the supply of bricks and pavers made by a range of manufacturers. Some also deal with other masonry materials and roof tiles. They do not hold stocks, but frequently have a 'library' of sample bricks to give choice and assist selection. They have an extensive knowledge of what is available and many can offer expertise in finding bricks to match existing brickwork. Acting as an intermediary between customers and manufacturers, they quote prices, take orders, negotiate customers' special requirements and arrange deliveries to site.

Names of local brick factors are listed in *Yellow Pages* directories under 'Brick suppliers' and under 'Builders' supplies'.

Builders merchants are dealers in all materials, components and equipment required in construction work. They hold stocks of some popular facing bricks and pavers, but will also take orders for other bricks described in manufacturers' literature and for special shaped bricks. They can be expected to have manufacturers' literature and many have a 'library' of sample bricks. Builders merchants can offer account facilities and have transport for delivery. Names of local builders merchants are listed in *Yellow Pages* directories. Alternatively the Builders Merchants Federation will be able to provide contact details of their members (*see* Useful Contacts).

DIY Supermarkets/Superstores primarily supply retail customers and small builders with building materials from stock on display on a cash and carry basis. Orders for non-stocked supplies are not normally invited. The choice of bricks and pavers is very limited. The fact that they can be bought in very small quantities, even singly, makes this source of supply very expensive and only appropriate for small quantities.

Mortar Materials

Builder's merchants supply all the constituents to make mortars. Cements, lime and dry packed mortar mixes are sold in stout paper sacks and will be branded products. The sand (builder's, bricklayer's or mortar sand) is sold loose in bulk by weight or by volume measured in cubic metres and fractions of cubic metres. It might be offered in large non-returnable woven polypropylene bags.

Mortar plasticizers are branded products and may be in liquid or powder form. Colour pigments are branded products in powder form; choice might be limited from stock, but a range of colour may be ordered.

Lime/sand 'ready mix' for mortar and retarded 'ready to use' mortar, with colouring pigment if required, are delivered direct to site by specialist suppliers. Contact ready-mixed concrete companies listed in *Yellow Pages* directories under 'Concrete – ready-mixed'. Although it is not always indicated in their display notices, they also supply mortars. Alternatively the Mortar Industries Association will be able to provide contact details (*see* Useful Contacts).

Reclaimed Bricks and Pavers

Local suppliers of reclaimed building materials can be found in *Yellow Pages* directories under listings of 'Architectural salvage', 'Builder's merchants' and/or 'Salvage & reclamation'.

SALVO!, an organization promoting the re-use of reclaimed building materials, can provide regional lists of specialist dealers (*see* Useful Contacts).

CHAPTER 3

Bricklaying

TOOLS AND EQUIPMENT

A bricklayer, like many craft specialists, acquires many tools as different tasks stimulate a need for them. However, there are a few tools that are essential for building basic brickwork. None are very expensive and if care is taken of them, and they are cleaned after use, they will last for many years.

Trowels

The traditional pattern of the British bricklaying trowel has a kite-shaped steel blade. One of its two long edges is straight and the other slightly curved. These trowels are available right- or left-handed and are referred to as the 'London' pattern. The straight edge is the working edge and is straight so that the proper alignment of one brick on another can be 'felt' as it is laid. The other edge is hardened to resist damage when it is used to tap bricks down or rough cut them. They vary slightly in size. Larger sizes are less easy to manage and can be tiring for inexperienced users. A trowel with a blade of 260 × 110mm (10½ × 4½in) is recommended for amateur use.

An American trowel, the Marshalltown 'Philadelphia' pattern is also widely available in the UK. It is broader than the 'London' pattern and is symmetrical with slightly curved edges. It is able to lift more mortar, which makes it more suitable for laying wide concrete blocks.

Pointing trowels, small symmetrical kite-shaped trowels with straight edges, are made with blade lengths of 50, 75, 100 and 150mm (2, 3, 4 and 6in). They are much more manageable for pointing, but also useful for filling any incidental holes in joints

when bricklaying. The 75 and 150mm sizes (3 and 6in) would be reasonable sizes to try first.

Spirit Levels

A 1200mm (4ft) long spirit level with bubble vials arranged to check horizontality and verticality is a convenient general purpose size. Aluminium alloy patterns are robust and stable in shape.

Bricks laid as soldiers, i.e. on end, look unsightly if they are not upright. A short spirit level about 200mm (8in) long is convenient to check the verticality of each one as it is placed.

Tape Measure and Pencil

A long retractable steel tape measure is suitable for setting out and checking work. A broad tape in a case with a trigger to hold the tape out, is a convenient type.

A pencil is used to make discrete mark on bricks, e.g. when plumbing perpends locations and marking bricks for cutting. Pencil is preferable to chalk, which is not easy to remove.

Line, Pins, Blocks and Tingle Plates

A line is used to stretch between the raised ends of straight brickwork to control alignment when laying a course of bricks or blocks. Twisted polypropylene, often orange or yellow to aid visibility, is a popular material as it is light, strong, waterproof and easily wiped clean. The twisting gives a very slight resilience, so that it holds the tension when pulled tight. Ordinary string absorbs water and tends to sag when wet.

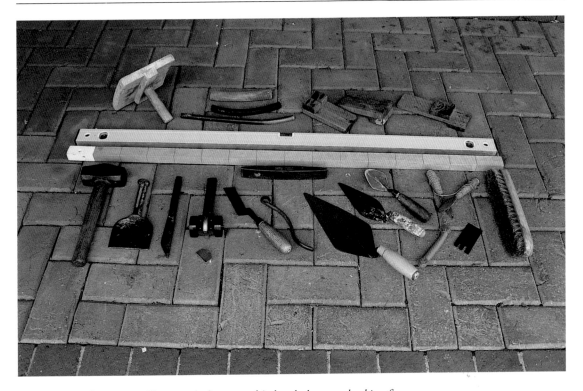

Bricklayers' tools. Top row (these can be home-made): hawk, hoses and tubing for use as jointing tools, pair of line blocks, gauge for marking bricks for accurate cutting (¼, ½, ¾); middle row: spirit level, gauge rod, boat level; bottom row: club hammer, bolster, plugging chisel, wheeled jointer (with alternative profile insert), square-edged jointer, 'bucket handle' jointer, London pattern trowel, pointing trowels, line, pair of line pins and line, tingle plate, soft bristle brush.

A pair of steel line pins are used to fasten the line. The pins are about 125mm (5in) long with large button heads and long flattened spear-shaped ends, which are pushed into the vertical joints between bricks. The ends of the line are wound onto pins, clockwise on one and anti-clockwise on the other, so that the line runs off the top edge of the flat pins.

As an alternative to pins, the line can be twisted into corner blocks that grip the end of brickwork and are held in position by the tension of the line. Traditionally they can be made from wood, but plastic versions are available.

To prevent a long line sagging, it can be given intermediate support with a tingle plate. This is a piece of thin metal or rigid plastic sheet approx. 75 × 25mm (3 × 1in) cut to form three fingers about

12mm (½in) long at one end. To use, set a brick to the correct height at an intermediate position and weigh the tingle down on it with the line held by running it between the fingers over the central one.

Jointers

Mortar joints can be formed in a variety of profiles, some of which require particular tools. Simple weather-struck profiles are formed to bed-joints with a standard trowel and to cross-joints (vertical joints) with a small pointing trowel.

To form a bucket handle profile there are purpose-made metal jointers available. A typical design is a cranked strip of steel with ends curved to give a choice of two depths of recess. Alternatively, a curved short length of 12mm bore copper tubing can be

Tooling a bucket handle joint profile.

used to form a similar profile. Metal tools tend to polish the surface of the mortar, which can give a hard unattractive appearance.

A short length of tough rubber hose of 20mm or 30mm diameter, as used on car engines, can give a very pleasant finish. Plastic garden hose tends to be too flexible and polishes the surface, and wooden mouldings wear too quickly and create an inconsistent profile.

Recessed joints are best finished using a wheeled jointer, colloquially called a 'chariot'. A good design has an adjustable pick to scrape out mortar to a consistent depth and a hardened steel adjustable slipper to firm the mortar surface within the recess. This type of jointer has alternative slippers to form other profiles.

Mortar Joint Profiles

The joints in brickwork affect its appearance by accentuating the form of individual bricks or merging them into an homogeneous surface. Colour is important, as is their profile, which may reveal or obscure the edges of the bricks. The profile also casts shadows and catches light to give characteristic effects.

A variety of joint profiles are used in brickwork. The most popular are 'bucket handle', 'weather struck', 'flush' and 'recessed'. All these profiles can be formed as the brickwork is laid, or afterwards by pointing the joints as a separate operation. Some profiles, e.g. 'weather struck and cut' are only practical as pointing.

As a brick is laid, mortar is squeezed from the bed-joint. When the brick is properly set in position, the excess mortar is skimmed off the surface to leave a flush joint. To do this, a trowel is held at an angle to the wall surface with the edge under the projecting mortar; it is then run forward along the line of the bed-joint to cut off the excess. The trowel blade should not be scraped up or down the face of the brickwork, as that will smear mortar onto the surface of the bricks. The mortar is then left to stiffen slightly.

The time taken for the mortar to reach the correct consistency is difficult to predict, as it is very variable, but start checking after about ten minutes. It must be stiff enough not to flow or adhere to tools, but not so stiff that it

Setting a brick to the line and cutting off mortar squeeze.

crumbles and breaks away if tools are applied to shape it.

If a 'flush' joint profile is wanted, no further working need be done on the bed-joints, but make good any cross-joints that might need a little more mortar and cutting them off flush to match the bed-joints.

The 'bucket handle' joint is formed with a half round or circular jointer as described on page 43. The end of the tool is used, pulling it along the joint in contact with the edges of the bricks on either side of the joint. Cross-joints are finished first and then the bed-joints.

Weather-struck joints are formed with trowels. The inset edge of the joint should not be exaggerated, 1–2mm is enough and the thickness of a trowel blade is a good guide. The forward edge should finish on the edge of the brick. Cross-joints are formed first. A small pointing trowel is held with its edge pressed into the mortar against one brick and drawn across the joint against the other. A right-handed bricklayer forms the inset on the left side. Either direction is correct, but make sure that the direction of the slope is the same throughout the work, if it is not the brickwork will look patchy. The bed-joints are formed with the straight edge of a normal trowel pressed into the mortar against the upper brick and, while holding it against the edge of the lower brick, pushing it along and down.

The 'weather-struck and cut' profile is formed as pointing. The inset edge is formed as with 'weather struck' but the forward edge is projected about a millimetre beyond the brick surface. It is cut straight using the edge of a pointing trowel for the cross-joints. The bed-joint projection is cut using a specially shaped knife called a 'Frenchman' and a straight edge with blocks to hold it off the wall surface.

Recessed joints are raked out to a consistent depth. The wheeled jointer described on page 44 is an effective tool for this. The raked profile can be left as finished, but it is better to compact the surface of the mortar to improve its resistance to rain penetration. For this a slipper iron in a wheeled jointer can be used or a square-edged bar jointer. Exaggerated recessing should be avoided, 5mm produces a good effect.

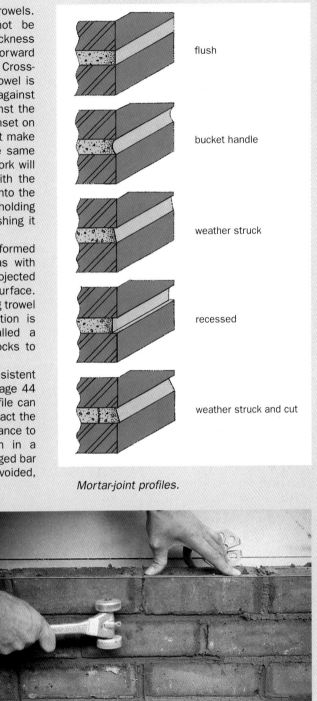

flush

bucket handle

weather struck

recessed

weather struck and cut

Mortar-joint profiles.

Wheeled jointer used for raking out mortar to form a recessed joint.

Brush

A soft bristle hand-brush is used to lightly brush the face of brickwork at the end of a session of work. Care should be taken not to leave brush marks in any mortar that is still soft.

Bolster and Club Hammer

Bricks can be cut to suit bonding arrangements using a heavy broad chisel called a bolster and a club hammer. A 100mm (4in) bolster and a 1.3kg (3lb) club hammer are suitable.

Spot Board

To hold small amounts of mortar within reach of the work, one or more spot boards are used. The boards are typically plywood, about 600mm (2ft) square and are generally raised on a few bricks to reduce stooping.

Gauge and Storey Rods

Consistency of the width of bed-joints is important for the good appearance of brickwork and 'keeping the gauge' is a very essential part of bricklaying. Regular checks must be made and a gauge rod is an invaluable aid.

A gauge rod is made from a straight, planed timber lath – typically 50 × 25mm nominal (2 × 1in). For small constructions a length of about 1500mm (5ft) is convenient, but for a building make a rod that slightly exceeds the height of a storey.

The ends must be square and undamaged. Select the best to be the 'working' end and clearly mark the other end 'TOP'. From the 'working' end make pencil marks every 300mm, then subdivide each of these lengths into four 75mm increments. Using a woodworking square, carefully 'square off' the pencil marks across the wide face of the lath and around onto one edge. Ideally these marks should be made permanent using a fine saw, but scoring with a ball-point pen will be reasonably serviceable. The dimensions quoted are for standard gauge using metric standard bricks, but if bricks of another size are to be used, or different gauge, the rod would be marked appropriately for that job.

If a storey rod is made, salient points such as the heights of walls, window and door heads and sills, corbels and other features are indicated by arrow-heads and an abbreviated identification. If there are several heights to be indicated, it might be considered preferable to transfer the particular dimensions onto the back face of the rod and mark them there.

In use the rod is placed on a reference point, typically a nail or wooden block temporarily fixed at DPC level at the base of a wall, to check that each course is placed at the correct level. It is also used to check that door and window frames are supported at the right height, so that they are built into the brickwork with their the heads at the correct level.

A vertical gauge rod is an essential tool. One made to horizontal gauge is a great help in setting out too, but if the job is not very large, a tape measure can be used. A horizontal gauge rod is prepared by transferring dimensions 225, 450, 675, 900 and so on up to 1800mm (i.e. in 225mm increments) from a tape measure and marking them permanently, as described above.

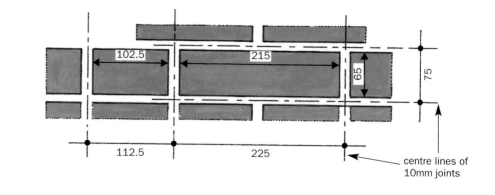

Diagram of co-ordinating sizes for brickwork.

DIMENSIONAL CO-ORDINATION AND BONDING

Justification of dimensions of standard bricks has been explained in Chapter 2. Although any dimensions can be accommodated by adjusting joint widths and/or cutting bricks, proper use of brickwork starts with organizing its dimensions to accord with the co-ordinated dimensions of bricks and the mortar joints between them.

The co-ordinating dimensions are based on each dimension of a brick plus the width of a joint (actually half-joints all around). The co-ordinating dimensions of a standard brick are listed in the table at the bottom of this page.

Vertical Gauge

There are small variations in the dimensions of individual bricks because of the way they are made. To allow for differences in height, bricks are laid with their top edges (arrises) aligned horizontally and therefore their lower edges may not be perfectly aligned and the thickness of the bed joint mortar will vary as a consequence. If the bricks are generally oversized or undersized, the bed-joints will be correspondingly thinner or thicker to compensate. This is correct. Consistent vertical gauge of 75mm increments takes precedence over bed-joint dimensions of 10mm. A gauge rod, or storey rod, is used to check that vertical gauge is being maintained.

The comments about using brickwork cladding to timber-frame construction in Chapter 4 include notes regarding the possible need for adjusting vertical gauge when cladding more than one storey.

Lintels to openings must bear on brickwork bed-joints and so the heights of door and window frames should co-ordinate with the 75mm increments. If they are to be built in as the brickwork is erected, their tops should be positioned at the correct height (a storey rod is used for this) and the frame supported by packing below. If a frame height does not co-ordinate with the 75mm gauge, adjustments should be done immediately below the sill. Bricks can be cut thinner as a split course, or a course of headers laid on edge (equivalent of 1½ normal courses) can look a neat alternative.

Horizontal Gauge

Co-ordination of horizontal dimensions is more complicated because of the overlapping of bricks in the different bond patterns and the need to keep the overall pattern consistent. Where possible, brickwork dimensions of whole-brick increments (225mm) should be used, i.e. 450, 675, 900, 1125mm. This applies to overall dimensions and to the widths of openings and the lengths of brickwork between them. Whole brick increments allow the lengths of brickwork to be set out symmetrically. For example, in the photograph on page 48 each end of any course is a mirror image of the other, and comparing the jambs of the window opening at each level there is either a header (a half-brick or the end of a brick) matched with a header, or a stretcher (a whole brick length) matched with a stretcher. See also the photograph on page 49 where this is not the case and headers are opposite stretchers.

Although half-bricks (headers) are used in all bond patterns, albeit only at the ends of walls and adjacent to openings in stretcher bond, brickwork lengths corresponding to whole- and half-brick lengths, e.g. 562, 787, 1012, 1237mm, the bricks cannot be

Co-ordinating dimensions for brickwork using standard bricks		
Brick size (mm)	Mortar joint (mm) (5mm all round)	Co-ordinating dimensions (mm)
Length = 215	10	225
Width = 102.5	10	112.5
Height = 65	10	75

Co-ordinated dimensions – overall, openings and panels.

(a) A bricklayer will often place broken bond centrally

(b) Alternatively three-quarter bats at each end can be used

(c) Reversing the bond at each end of the wall is not symetrical, but does avoid cut bricks

Alternative ways to deal with bonding when overall dimension includes a half increment.

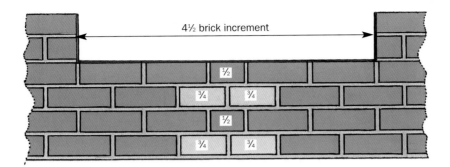

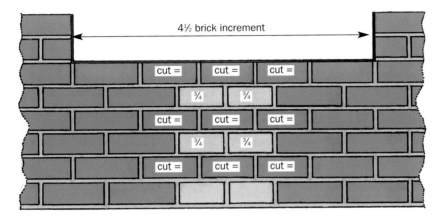

The visual impact of broken bond can be reduced by cutting extra bricks so that none are less than three-quarters long.

arranged symmetrically and therefore the bonding is imperfect. Often the use of cut bricks is necessary to modify the bond pattern to suit dimensions that are not of brick increments. Such arrangements are known as 'broken bond'.

If dimensions of whole-brick increments are not practicable, various alternative arrangements are possible. Some may be considered preferable to others. Before starting to lay brickwork, check the dimensions and how the bricks will be bonded in alternate courses. This can be done on paper (squared paper is a help) or with a dry assembly of bricks beforehand. By identifying any problem areas before work commences, alternative solutions can be explored and the best one chosen. Never start bricklaying in the hope that it will sort itself out.

Reverse bond across reveals avoids broken bond above and below opening with half increment.

Many bond patterns are used in brickwork. The more common ones are described in Chapter 4. English bond has courses entirely of stretchers and so, even though there are courses entirely of headers, it is preferable to use dimensions of whole-brick increments.

Flemish bond has headers and stretchers in each course and the pattern shifts three-quarters of a brick in alternate courses. For large areas it can be very attractive, but maintaining consistency of the bond pattern in narrow panels and incorporating openings without disturbing the bond in the brickwork above and below them requires careful pre-planning.

Piers, Openings and Recesses

When deciding upon dimensions allow for missing or extra joints. The co-ordinating size of 225mm includes joints, but there is one less joint than the number of bricks in the width of a pier and one more in the width of an opening or a recess. This is illustrated in the figure below. The cross-joints in the

pier shown in the figure on page 51 are much wider than normal because the nominal width of 450mm includes 10mm for a joint that is not present. The effect is obvious, and unattractive. In a recess of the same nominal width, the joints would be narrower to make room for the extra joint. It is preferable to size such features related to actual number of bricks and joints, rather than to use nominal dimensions.

In straight runs of more than, say, seven brick increments, adjustment of joint widths to accommodate 10mm more or less is unlikely to be noticeable.

Setting Out

It is important to set out the position, alignment and squareness of the proposed brickwork accurately, as it cannot be adjusted later.

Generally all brickwork should be constructed level and vertical, therefore new foundations or an existing base should be suitably prepared to allow for this. Some structures may be isolated and their exact relationship with other features on the site may not

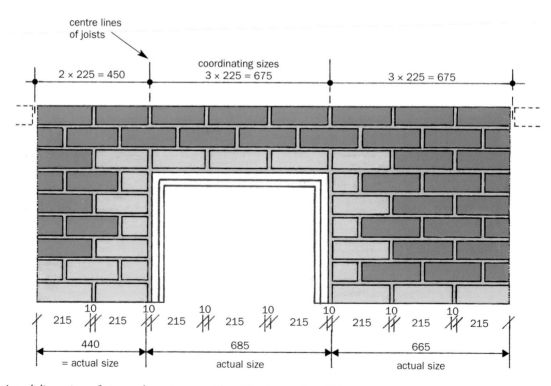

Actual dimensions of piers and openings are affected by the number of joints.

be critical, e.g. for an isolated raised bed in a garden or retaining wall to replace an earth bank. Other constructions, such as boundary walls or extensions to existing buildings, will require very precise setting out, both horizontally and vertically, to relate new levels to existing ones. The setting-out methods described in the following notes will not be appropriate for all brickwork projects.

Setting Out on Plan

Normal building practice is to set out the outline of the external face of the structure using string lines between nails fixed to 'profile boards'. These are horizontal boards – typically 75 × 25mm (3 × 1in) – and in length a little wider than the wall be constructed, and fixed to pairs of stout pegs driven into the ground about 2m (6ft 6in) beyond the corners being plotted, i.e. clear of the area to be disturbed by the construction. Profile boards are more stable than a

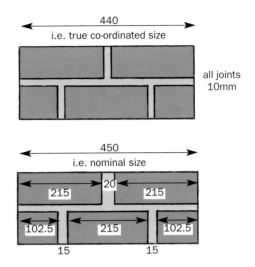

A pier set out to a nominal size will have unattractive, thick cross-joints.

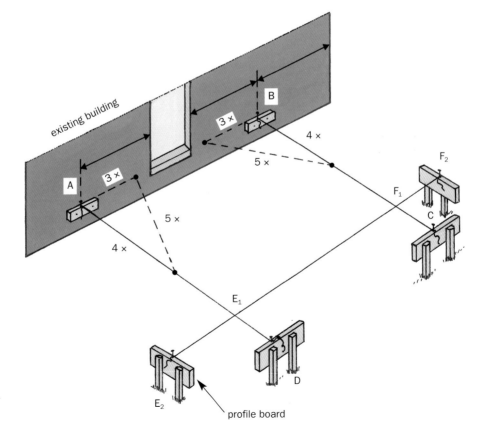

Setting-out using profile boards.

single peg that, if subsequently knocked, could easily lead to inaccuracies. The boards should be fixed level and at approximately in the same height.

The area affected should be cleared of topsoil and loose material. The figure on page 51 illustrates a typical arrangement. Two people can set this up as follows:

1. Plot points A and B with reference to the existing structure and define their positions with nails driven into mortar joints or profile boards fixed to the wall.
2. Set up lines B/C and A/D at a right angles to A/B and fix by nails at C and D. A triangle with sides three, four and five units long has a right angle opposite the longest side. This fact can be used to set up these lines.
3. Measure off the required dimensions A/E1 and B/F1 and mark with a piece of string tied around lines.
4. Pull line through E1 and F1 and fix to nails at E2 and F2.
5. Check for squareness – dimension A/F1 should be the same as B/E1.

Using the lines, the corners positions can be transferred to the ground below by plumbing down and marking with a small peg with a nail in the top. Lines offset from these reference points can then be used to set out the foundations. It is not practical to follow string lines with a mechanical digger and so dry cement or lime is used to mark their width on the ground.

The string lines can now be taken off the profile boards while the foundations are dug and laid. They can then be refixed to set out the brickwork.

Checking and Setting Out Levels

For extensions to existing buildings, new structures must be built at the correct level so that floors relate to one another as anticipated. If a suitable permanent reference point is not convenient to the new work, it is normal to set one up (a datum point) within easy reach of the brickwork to be built, so that the top of the foundation, courses of brickwork and openings for doors and windows are built at the correct level in relation to the existing building.

An optical level or theodolite and target staff could be used to survey existing levels and set up datum levels, but they are not essential. A long cased spirit level, at least 1200mm (4ft), can be used with a long, straight, parallel edged board to extend its reach.

A water level is a simple but effective tool that is easy to make. It consists of a length of garden hose with short lengths of clear tubing at each end. The ends are stopped when not in use. If there are no air

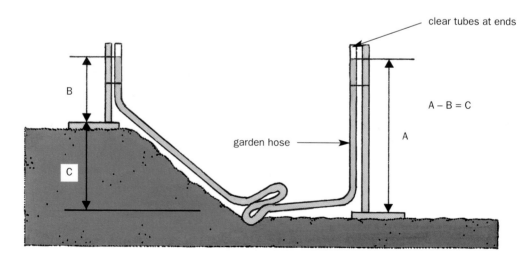

Using a water level.

locks or kinks in the hose, the water in the clear tubes at each end will be at the same level – provided that the end tubes are open, are at a similar height and are higher than the rest of the hose.

To measure differences in level, hold the ends of the tubing above the surfaces to be compared and measure the distance between the water level in each tube and the surface below it. The difference between the two measurements is the difference in level of the surfaces. A water level is particularly useful when the levels to be compared, or set out, are a long distance apart, e.g. when setting out falls for paving.

BUILDING STRAIGHT WALLS

In most cases, brickwork will be straight and vertical with right-angled corners. The following notes assume this simple form.

Before commencing work with mortar, mark the positions of the corners of the brickwork on the top surface of the foundation. Between these points mark the locations of any piers and openings for windows and door that will be formed within the run of the wall, even though they might be required at a much higher level. This is to ensure that the piers and the reveals of the openings register properly with the bonding of the brickwork. Place bricks at pier and reveal positions and set out the rest of the brickwork dry to check that the various sections work to brick sizes correctly, noting any broken bond (or reverse bond) that might be necessary.

Building the Corners

Brickwork is built by constructing the corners or ends of the straight runs and 'lining in' the courses between them. The corners or ends must be built accurately, as any discrepancy will be reflected in the work that follows. Select well-shaped bricks for the work, so that the corners and ends will be square and precisely formed.

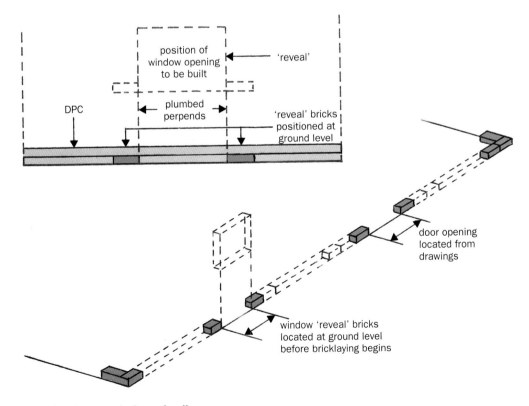

Setting-out reveal positions at the base of wall.

Pull lengths of bricklayer's line from the other corners of the walls that form the corner being built. At the corner wrap each line around a dry brick and place these about 200mm (8in) beyond the corner, but in line with it. The lines are for alignment only and should be lower than the top edges of the bricks being laid. With a trowel, lay a bed of mortar on the foundation to receive the corner brick. Assuming that the foundation top is at the correct level, and no adjustment of thickness of the bed-joint is required, press the corner brick into position using the lines as guides. Using a gauge rod and spirit level,

carefully adjust the brick so that its top is 75mm above the foundation and is level along and across its surface.

From the corner brick, lay five other bricks to form a corner. Lay them to standard horizontal gauge and carefully levelled from the corner brick and aligned with the guide lines, which can then be removed.

Lay the next corner brick and, using the gauge rod, set its top at 150mm above the foundation. Using the spirit level, check that its faces are vertical and directly above the first corner brick, and then check that the top is level in both directions. Lay four more

Laying the Bricks

Bricks are laid on a bed of mortar placed on the top of the course below. Spread a length of mortar for about three or four bricks. The quantity will come by practice, but the thickness should be about 16mm (⅝in) so that the bricks can be pressed down to gauge. The trowel can be drawn down the centre of the bed to form a shallow furrow and spread the mortar to the edges. Press the brick into the mortar. Align and level it using a bricklayer's line or spirit level and gauge rod, as appropriate, and check alignment with adjacent bricks. The top of the brick can be tapped down using the shoulder of the trowel opposite its working edge. To avoid chipping do not tap on the edge of the face of a brick.

If the bricks are very dry, and have a high water absorption, they may suck water from the mortar very quickly, particularly in hot dry weather. This will stiffen the mortar and make it difficult to adjust the brick. To reduce the suction of the bricks, they should be 'docked' by dipping each brick in a bucket of water for about seven seconds then standing it on end to drain before use. Dock a couple of dozen or so bricks at a time. Do not soak the bricks or they will be too wet. Never dock dense bricks – they have low suction and must always been laid dry.

The vertical joints between the bricks (cross-joints) should be filled with mortar. To do this, 'butter' mortar on the end of the brick to be laid. As the brick is pressed down onto the bed-joint it should be squeezed against the brick already laid to give a solid joint. Small dabs of mortar placed

on the corners of the brick do not produce joints that give adequate resistance to rain penetration – the gap in the middle does not get filled from above when the bed-joint mortar is laid for the next course.

Buttering the end of a brick for a cross-joint.

The only exception to this advice is when building corners or the ends of walls. The method described above will push the corner brick out of position, therefore leave the joints against the corner brick open. Leave the corner brick undisturbed until the next course is to be laid and then, very carefully, pack mortar into the open joint from the top with the point of a trowel.

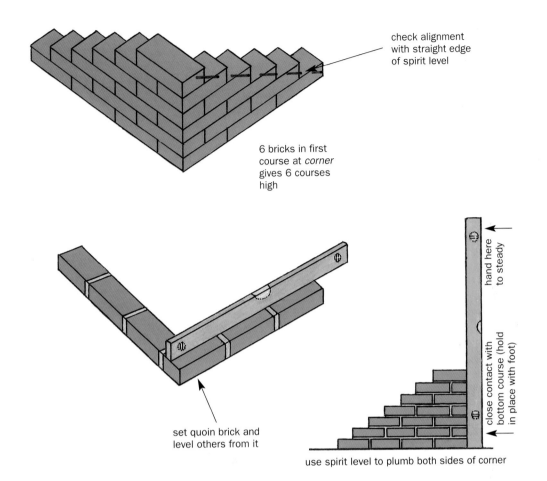

check alignment
with straight edge
of spirit level

6 bricks in first
course at *corner*
gives 6 courses
high

set quoin brick and
level others from it

hand here
to steady

close contact with
bottom course (hold
in place with foot)

use spirit level to plumb both sides of corner

Building a corner.

bricks to form the corner, checking each one for gauge, verticality, alignment and level. Continue to a height of six courses. This is the optimum height – there is no advantage in building higher. Check the whole assembly again for accuracy. Build the other corner or end.

The levels may be such that within the six courses a DPC will need to be built in. If this is the case, because the DPC material is sandwiched between two thin beds of mortar, the joint is very likely to be slightly thicker than 10mm, perhaps 12 or 13mm. In anticipation, to compensate for this, the courses below the DPC could be laid very slightly low to gauge. The DPC should be rolled up for later

continuation. The DPC at the other end of the wall will be treated similarly. Later, when lining-in the brickwork, the DPCs should be joined be lapping the ends 150mm.

If a cavity wall is being built, the corner of the outer leaf is built as described and then the corner of the inner leaf is built, generally blockwork. The inner face is set out from the outer face of the brickwork, i.e. the overall width of the cavity wall is the relevant dimension. It is convenient to mark the location of the internal corner on the foundation when the first course of the external leaf has been laid. Build the inner leaf accurately as errors will be detrimental to following work.

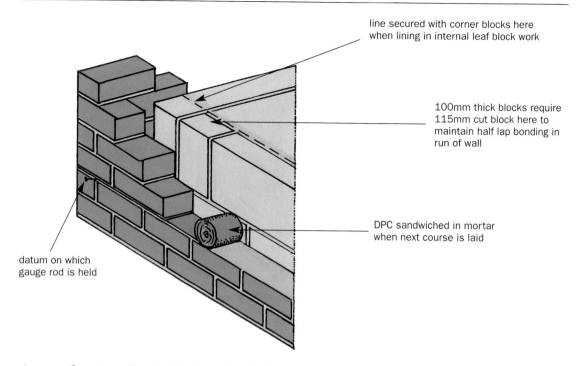

line secured with corner blocks here when lining in internal leaf block work

100mm thick blocks require 115mm cut block here to maintain half lap bonding in run of wall

DPC sandwiched in mortar when next course is laid

datum on which gauge rod is held

A corner of a cavity wall with a blockwork inner leaf.

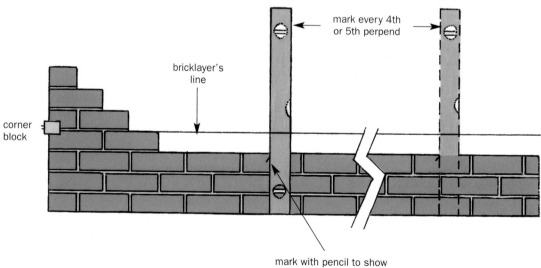

mark every 4th or 5th perpend

bricklayer's line

corner block

mark with pencil to show place of brick in next course

Lining-in brickwork between corners.

Lining-In

When corners, or ends, have been built, the brickwork in between can be 'lined-in', i.e. laid in courses guided by a bricklayer's line run from each end of the walling. The line is wound around either flat bladed pins pushed into mortar cross-joints, or corner blocks held on the vertical corner of the brickwork by the tension of the taut line. In either case, the line is set so that its top is in line with the top edges of the bricks in the course being laid and, when viewed from above, it should just be possible to see light between the line and the edges of the brick – they must not touch. As noted when describing tools, a tingle plate can be used to support a long line if it tends to sag.

The line is used to control the line and level of the bricks being laid, and its positioning dictates the vertical gauge. With the straight edge of the trowel blade, the bricklayer can 'feel' the alignment of the edges of the bricks. The line and trowel together allow bricks to be properly positioned without constant vertical and horizontal checks with the level

and gauge rod. Nevertheless, when a course has been completed, some checks with the spirit level are worthwhile before the line is raised to lay the next course.

The bricks should be evenly spaced throughout the length of the wall. There will be some small variation in the length of individual bricks and compensation for that will be made by varying of the width of the joints between them. In good brickwork the joints between bricks in a course should be consistent, but not necessarily exactly 10mm.

As noted in the comments on setting out, the positions of reveals to openings should be marked on the foundation and bricks set in these positions (*see* figure on page 53). At these points, the brickwork joints should be plumbed vertical as each course is laid, so that when the openings occur higher up the wall, the bonding will accommodate them without disruption. Between the positions bricks should be spaced evenly.

Any broken bond necessary should be consistent throughout the height of the brickwork, even if

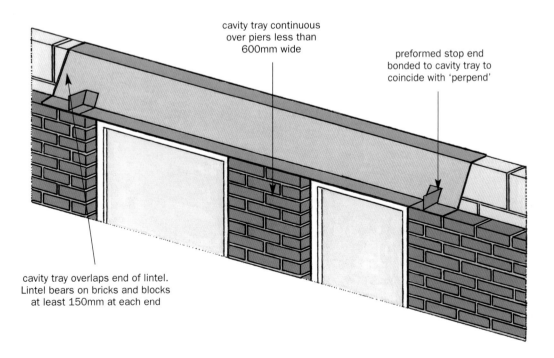

cavity tray continuous over piers less than 600mm wide

preformed stop end bonded to cavity tray to coincide with 'perpend'

cavity tray overlaps end of lintel. Lintel bears on bricks and blocks at least 150mm at each end

Cavity tray with stop ends and lintels over openings.

Full-fill insulation batts.

interrupted by openings. Cut bricks in broken bonds should be neat, consistent and plumbed vertical. Broken bonds tends to attract the eye, but it is less obvious if it is neat and well-aligned.

Ideally, joints between bricks in a course, cross-joints, should line through vertically with those in alternate courses. This is referred to as 'keeping the perps upright'. 'Perps' are the notional lines that run through cross-joints in alternate courses on the surface of brickwork – in good work they should be perpendicular, i.e. vertical. To call a cross-joint a 'perp' is a common misuse of the term.

Because bricks can vary slightly in length, it is not practical for every 'perp' to be plumb vertical. But if

Partial-fill insulation boards.

no control is exercised, erratic alignment can produce an unattractive disorderly appearance. By plumbing the 'perps' every fourth or fifth brick along the wall, and spacing the bricks with even joints in the intervals between them, a well-controlled appearance is achieved – the figure on page 56 indicates the procedure.

Cavity Walls

If a cavity wall is being laid, then the inner and outer leaves should be raised alternately, so that they give mutual support and bed-joints are levelled across the width of the whole wall. Lintels bear on both leaves and so their coursing must coincide, and wall ties should be level across the cavity and not slope downwards to the inner leaf.

Either leaf can lead. Where the choice is optional, raising the outer leaf first is preferable because the inner surface (in the cavity) can then be cleaned of

any excessive mortar squeezed from joints and any holes in the mortar can be filled. This is a particular advantage when full-fill cavity insulation is to be built in. The insulation is placed against the outer leaf and is normally held in place between the wall ties without special fittings. The inner leaf is then built up. Because the cavity is full of insulation, debris cannot be dropped into it. Also, as blockwork has fewer mortar joints than brickwork, there is little risk of mortar squeezing into the cavity and causing problems.

Thermal insulation slabs or boards built in to partially fill the cavity are normally fixed to the inner leaf and therefore construction would lead with that leaf.

Keeping a cavity free of mortar droppings is helped by the use of cavity battens. These are softwood battens slightly narrower than the gap to be kept clear, generally 50mm (2in), with lifting wire at each

Board used to prevent mortar droppings falling in cavity or on insulation.

end. The batten is laid on the wall ties in the cavity and lifted out and wiped clean before being replaced on the row of ties for the next section of the wall.

When the leading leaf of a cavity wall is being built, boards approximately 2400mm long (8ft) and wide enough to cover the cavity are laid over the cavity supported on the wall ties to stop mortar dropping onto the insulation or into any cavity.

Avoid mortar squeezing into the cavity as bricks are laid. To help with this, when bedding mortar is spread on the leaf of a cavity wall, the trowel should

Curved free-standing wall.

be run along the cavity edge at an angle to form a chamfer on the mortar bed. With some practice, this shaping of the bed will allow bricks to be pressed into the mortar and spread it to fill the joint without it squeezing beyond the plane of the cavity face.

Wall ties must be built in as bricks and blocks are laid. On no account should they be pushed into mortar joints. The type of insulation to be installed, and the width of the cavity between the masonry leaves, will dictate particular types of wall ties; Chapter 4 discusses wall ties.

Partial fill insulation will require fixings to hold it in place. Fixings are often clipped to wall ties and there may also be independent fastenings. Insulation manufacturers will provide guidance on the fixings recommended for use with their products.

The joints between all types of cavity insulation (boards, slabs or batts) must be clean and closely butted or interlocked.

BUILDING CURVED BRICKWORK

Walls that are curved on plan can be built with standard bricks laid to the line of the curve. The joints between taper. The curved surface consists of a series of facets and its acceptability will depend on the degree of roughness caused by the faceting and the widths of the mortar cross-joints.

An aspect of faceting is the 'overhang' caused by the bonding overlap of bricks in consecutive courses. The 'overhang' is more pronounced with half-lap stretcher bonds and is at its greatest with curves of small radius.

In the exposed surface of the wall, the width of the tapered mortar joints between the bricks can be varied from the normal, nominal 10mm. In most situations, 16mm can be regarded as the upper limit in convex face work and 6mm the lower limit in concave face work. Joint profile of the cross-joints

Tile inserts used as an alternative to thick mortar joints in curved capping.

needs to be considered – flush or very shallow bucket handle profiles generally being the most satisfactory. The textural character of the brick also has an influence.

Guidance on the minimum radii for curved walls of different thickness and bond is given in the table on page 63.

More comprehensive guidance on this subject is contained in BDA Design Note 12: *The Design of Curved Brickwork*. It includes information about the range of standard curved bricks specified in BS 4729: *Bricks of Special Shapes and Sizes* for convex curved brickwork of six radii between 450 and 5400mm (18in and 18ft). Faceting and overhangs do not occur with these curved bricks.

Setting Out Curved Walls

From the design drawing, locate on site the point from which the radius of curvature is struck. Mark out and dig a foundation trench and place a foundation with a flat surface at the appropriate level. Set out the line of the curved face of brickwork as indicated in the figure on page 63, and lay the bricks dry to check the size of the cross-joints.

Plumbing points should be marked at about 1200mm (4ft) intervals around the curve. Levelling, plumbing and gauge should be checked at these points. If a template is used it should span between them.

Building the wall can be controlled using a trammel pivoted on a vertical steel rod or tube set at the striking point. It must be truly plumb and stabilized by temporarily concrete. The trammel is used to check the position and alignment of every brick. It is threaded on the steel rod and supported on a rubber band or tube clamp that is moved up the rod to

Minimum radii for curved brickwork using standard bricks

Bond pattern	Wall thickness	Minimum radius when the face work is:		
		Convex	Concave	Both surfaces
Stretcher bond	Half-brick	1.5m (5ft)	2.0m (6ft 6in)	3.0m (10ft)
Stretcher bond English bond	One-brick	3.5m (11ft 8in)	3.5m (11ft 8in)	4.5m (15ft)
Flemish bond	One-brick	2.5m (8ft 4in)	3.5m (11ft 8in)	4.0m (13ft 4in)
Header bond	One-brick	1.5m (5ft)	2.0m (6ft 6in)	2.5m (8ft 4in)

match the level of the course being laid in the figure bottom right.

Templates

Space restrictions often make the trammel method impractical, and setting out and controlling alignment is then done with a template cut to the curve required – a thin plywood board about 1200mm (4ft) that can be supported in one hand, spanning between plumbing points, while holding a trowel in the other hand.

For a convex wall, both ends of each brick face must touch the template. For a concave wall, where a reverse template is used, the centre of the face of each brick must touch the template, with its ends equidistant from it.

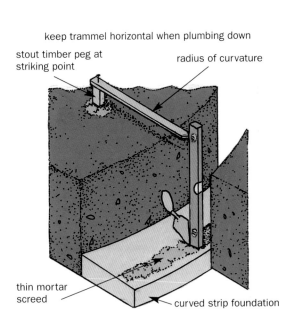

Setting out a curve from a striking point.

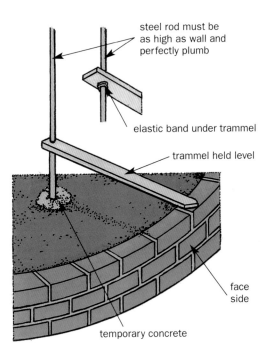

Trammel used to control building curved brickwork.

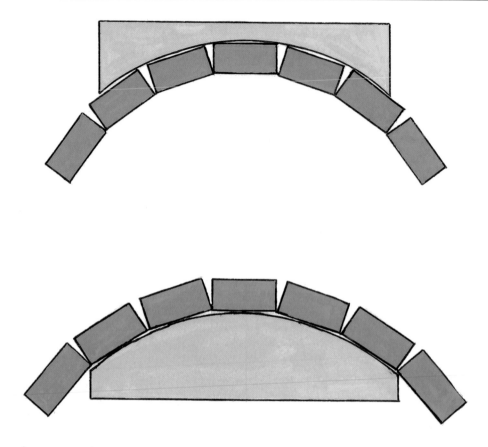

Convex and concave templates.

Laying the Bricks

Bed the first course of bricks to the line of the radius marked on the foundation. Use the trammel and spirit level to check alignment or the template spanned between the plumbing points. Any kinks in the first course will be continued to the full height of the wall. Level-in the bricks using a spirit level, with a straight edge if necessary to span between plumbing points.

Like corners in straight walls, plumbing points control plumb, gauge and alignment for the full height of a curved wall. Levelling of courses is done across, and with reference to, the plumbing points because that is where gauge is controlled (*see* the figure top left on page 65). Perpends should be plumbed at these points too.

BUILDING CURVED ARCHES

Arches can be built with standard bricks or special tapered bricks. In either case, careful setting-out and accurate alignment are essential for good appearance. The following notes refer to simple, single, curved arches, but the principles also apply to more complex shaped arches often seen in older brick buildings.

Rough Arches

Rough arches are built from standard, parallel-sided bricks with tapered mortar joints. The larger the radius, the less the joints taper. Rough arches are normally only used for semi-circular or segmental shapes (part of a semi-circle). If the radius of curvature is small, they are probably more acceptable if

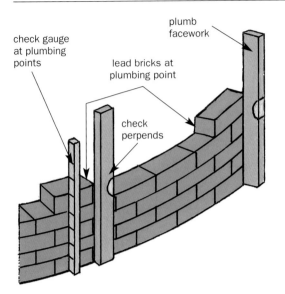

check gauge at plumbing points

lead bricks at plumbing point

plumb facework

check perpends

Checking gauge, plumb and perps at control points.

built with rugged, stock-type bricks, rather than with smooth, regular types.

Rough arches are most often in headers. For large spans they may be of two or more rings.

Gauged Arches

Gauged arches are built with tapered bricks (also called voussoirs). The mortar joints are parallel-sided. Traditionally, tapered bricks were cut from standard bricks by the bricklayer, but many brick manufacturers now supply sets to suit a selection of popular spans. Sets can also be made to order for specific requirements. British Standard BS 4729: *Bricks of Special Shapes and Sizes* specifies tapered headers and tapered stretchers for semi-circular arches for openings four, six, eight and twelve bricks wide.

Joints may be 10mm wide of normal mortar or they may be 2–3mm joints using lime putty joints to simulate traditional fine gauged brickwork.

Rough arch extended to form a bull's eye opening.

Gauged multiple-ring arch.

Centring

The underside of an arch needs centring as a support during construction. It is placed on folding wedges and timber props within the opening. The support must be strong and secure enough to bear the weight of the arch bricks without moving. The wedges allow adjustment when setting up and removal when the arch is finished and the mortar has gained strength. Centring must be perfectly plumb on face before setting the arch bricks.

In cavity walls, cavity trays are not as easily accommodated with arches as they are with flat lintels. Some steel lintel manufactures produce lintels with curved soffits that overcome this problem and act as permanent centres for brick arches.

Constructing a Rough Arch

1. Prepare the centring and secure it in the opening.
2. Plumb up from the striking point to locate the centre of the key (central) brick. Mark the width of the key brick in pencil on the centring and mark a joint allowance each side.

3. With a flexible tape, measure down the centring (the arch intrados) from the key brick to the springing line and divide into a whole number of equal-sized brick spaces, including a joint allowance, which should be as small as possible to avoid the tapered joints widening too much at the outer curved surface (the extrados). In practice the minimum joint using cement:sand mortars is 6mm.
4. Set the first arch brick at the springing line on a bedding of mortar built up slightly thicker at the extrados in order to form a wedge shaped joint.
5. Continue placing bricks on wedge-shaped bedding mortar to follow the curve. Build up both sides alternately so that the centring is loaded evenly. Check that the centre lines of the bricks and of the mortar joints align with a string stretched from the striking point of the curve to the outer curve of the arch.
6. Set each brick accurately to the pencil marks and square across the soffit.

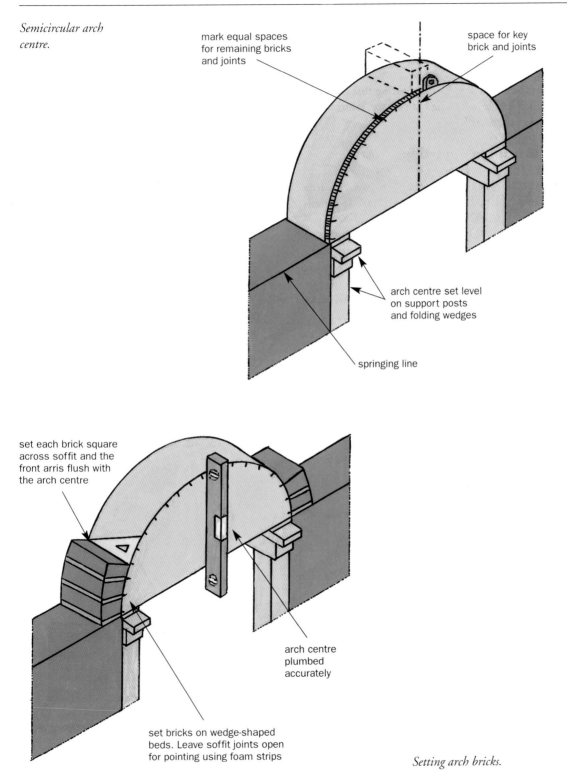

Semicircular arch centre.

mark equal spaces for remaining bricks and joints

space for key brick and joints

arch centre set level on support posts and folding wedges

springing line

set each brick square across soffit and the front arris flush with the arch centre

arch centre plumbed accurately

set bricks on wedge-shaped beds. Leave soffit joints open for pointing using foam strips

Setting arch bricks.

7. Keep the centring free of mortar by bedding back and leaving a joint space for pointing later. Foam or wood strips can be inserted at the soffit to assist this.

8. Set the key brick in place ensuring that mortar is solidly packed into the last two top joints at the crown of the arch.

Constructing a Gauged Segmental Arch

Segmental indicates that the curve is part of a true circle but less than a half circle (semicircle). In a semi-circular arch, the end bearings (springing) are horizontal. In a segmental arch, they are at an angle and the bearing position in the wall is cut to a corresponding angle (skewback) to receive them. The following description assumes tapered bricks (voussoirs) are used and that the skewbacks have been formed accurately.

1. Set up a temporary arch support as before. Also set up, wedged in the opening below, a board with a nail at the striking point of the arch's radius. An arch setting-out drawing prepared by the designer or the brick manufacturer should have the necessary dimensions for the centring, arch radius, skewback angle and joint widths.

2. Plumb up from the striking point to locate the centre of the key brick. Mark the width of the key brick on the top of the centring with a pencil.

3. Mark a joint space, as shown on the arch drawing, at each side of the key brick space.

4. Mark out in pencil the required number of spaces each side of the key brick corresponding to the number of voussoirs in the arch. Each space includes one joint.

5. Bed the first voussoir at the springing of the arch (on an even bed of mortar) and check joint alignment using a piece of string fixed to the striking point of the arch. Continue bedding and checking voussoirs. Work alternately on each side so as to load the centring evenly.

6. Keep the soffit joints clear of mortar for later pointing as previously described.

7. Ensure voussoirs are square on the soffit and follow pencil markings precisely. Check the alignment of joints with the string from the striking point.

8. Constantly check face plane alignment with a straight edge, or line and pins.

9. When it becomes impractical to apply mortar to the previously laid brick 'butter' each voussoir evenly across the bedding surface before setting.

10. Complete with key brick, jointing as indicated in the figure on page 69.

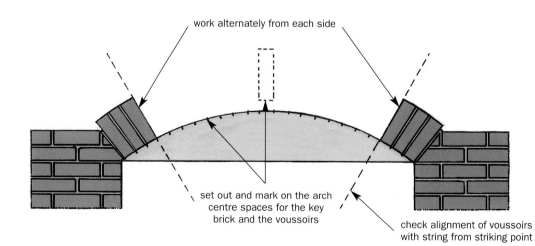

work alternately from each side

set out and mark on the arch centre spaces for the key brick and the voussoirs

check alignment of voussoirs with string from striking point

Setting out a segmental gauged arch.

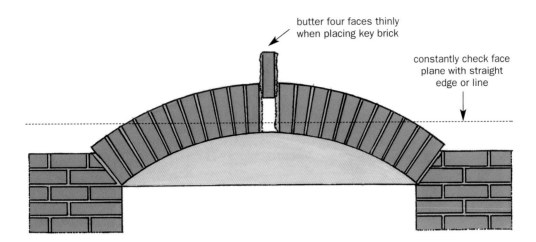

Completing the arch.

CHAPTER 4

Brickwork Masonry

THE APPEARANCE OF BRICKWORK

Probably the most important reason for the popularity of brickwork is its attractive appearance. The choice of brick is fundamental to the visual character of brickwork, but the joints and the bonding arrangement of the bricks also profoundly affect the overall look of the brickwork.

If existing brickwork is being extended or repaired, it is obvious that bricks for the new work should match the colour, texture and size of the existing ones as closely as possible. Not so obvious, but of equal importance, is the need to match the colour, texture, size and finish of the mortar joints, and also the bond pattern of the work.

The choice of bricks is very extensive. They vary from pale buff, through yellow, red, purple, brown, grey to blue/black. Some are multi-coloured. Surface textures range from rough, partially distorted with deep crease marks, through fine, dimpled or scratched textures, to smooth shiny surfaces. Some bricks are very regular, with sharp, straight, well-formed arrises and are relatively consistent in size. Others have minor distortions and are not precisely formed; they are somewhat irregular and, although they conform to standard tolerances, their dimensions vary. These variations lead to characteristic appearances in the build work and require the exercise of appropriate craft skills to achieve the best results.

The coloration of bricks has a natural variation and it is normal good practice to blend them as they are laid. If more than one pack of bricks is used for a job, three or more should be opened and bricks taken from them at random in order to give a good mix.

When matching existing bricks take care to match their original colour and disregard changes due to stains or weathering. If the new brickwork appears too fresh and pristine there are techniques to tone it down and accelerate the effects of weathering (see Chapter 6).

Although mortar joints appear as narrow lines, the total surface area of the mortar is a surprisingly large proportion of the whole brickwork surface. With stretcher bond, only the long faces of the bricks are seen and the number of mortar joints are minimized, nevertheless over 17 per cent of the surface area of the brickwork is mortar. When there are headers in a bond pattern, there are more joints and the surface area of mortar increases. In English bond about 20 per cent of the surface area is mortar. In curved work using all headers the proportion can be as high as 25 per cent.

These large proportions help to explain the surprising effect mortar colour has on brickwork appearance. A dark-toned mortar will tend to make the bricks themselves appear darker and richer in colour. Conversely a light-coloured mortar will make the bricks appear lighter, as if some of their colour has been drawn from them.

Strongly coloured mortar will create a colour bias in the brickwork. For example, a red-coloured mortar will enhance the redness of a red brick, or give a warm tone to a buff one.

Mortar joints should be finished at the surface with a consistently shaped profile. Each profile casts a characteristic shadow in sunlight and this has an effect on appearance. A recessed joint casts a dense, bold shadow and darkens the tone of the brickwork

Attractive brickwork using three different bricks.

by the darkness in the joint. Conversely a flush joint casts no shadow and gives a more homogeneous feeling to the masonry. The concave surface of a bucket-handle joint creates a soft shadow at each bed joint.

The colour and texture of the mortar and the profile of the joint finish should be chosen with care and bricklaying must achieve consistent results.

BONDING PATTERNS

Traditional brickwork is generally robust with a thickness no less than the length of a brick and generally much greater. A bricklayer referring to brickwork dimensions often expresses them in increments of brick lengths, e.g. 'one-brick wall', 'one-and-a-half-brick wall', 'two-brick pier', which refer to the dimensions 215mm, 327mm and 440mm (nominally 9, 13½ and 18in). This is because brickwork dimensions are determined by brick sizes and consistent mortar-joint thickness. Working within the constraints of a regularized system minimizes the need for cutting bricks and maintains a neat appearance.

When bricks are laid together, they are placed so that vertical joints, which show in the face of the brickwork, do not align in adjacent courses, and continuous vertical joints within the thickness of the work are avoided or kept to a minimum. This integrated arrangement, known as 'bonding', promotes the even distribution of forces applied to the brickwork by the elements it supports, such as floors, beams, roofs.

In some early medieval brickwork, the dimensions of the bricks are not very consistent and, although they are overlapped, there is no systematic arrangement. Such work is described as being laid in haphazard bond. Bricks made to reasonably consistent dimensions can be laid in regular bonding arrangements. The repetitive nature of bonding

The effect of different mortar colour on the same brick in a demonstration panel (see *the photograph on page 30*).

creates distinctive patterns in the face of brickwork and there are a number of established configurations, but most are variations of one of three basic bonding arrangements: English bond, Flemish bond and stretching, or stretcher, bond.

English and Flemish bonds are used in brickwork of one brick or more thick. Some of the bricks are placed with their stretchers (long faces) parallel to the surface of the work; the others are placed at right angles so that their headers (ends) appear in the surface of the brickwork, and they lap over and bond with bricks behind the surface. Bonds are distinguished by the pattern of stretchers and headers that appear in the surface of the brickwork.

In English bond, courses of stretchers alternate with courses of headers. It is the oldest pattern and in some other countries is known as ancient bond. Because there are no continuous vertical joints within

the thickness of the brickwork it is regarded as the strongest bonding arrangement. The visual contrast of courses of headers with courses of stretchers tends to emphasize horizontality, and with differences of colour or tone between headers and stretchers it can sometimes have a marked, striped appearance. English bond and variations based on it were used for all brickwork of one brick or more thick until the introduction of Flemish bond in the mid-seventeenth century.

To provide decoration in the form of cross and diamond-shaped motifs and diaper patterns, modifications to the normal form of English bond are often seen and headers of a contrasting colour are included.

Flemish bond has stretchers and headers alternately in each course and is regarded as having a more refined appearance. There is neither horizontal nor vertical emphasis in the surface pattern. Because of its

The effect of joint profile on appearance. Same brick throughout, but with flush joints in top panel and recessed joints below.

superior appearance, Flemish bond is very widely used. Its internal bonding arrangement does allow narrow continuous vertical joints parallel to the wall surface and, theoretically, this weakens the bond. For this reason, English bond continues to be the preferred bond for brickwork bridges, viaducts, embankment walls and other civil engineering work.

English bond – in this example the colour difference between headers and stretchers emphasizes the horizontal character of this pattern.

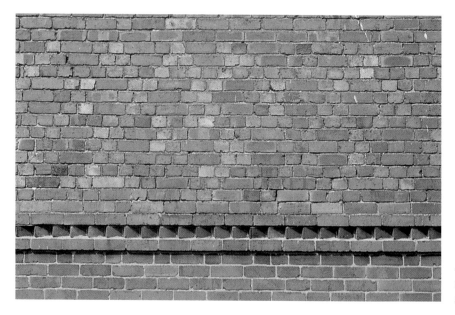

Diaper patterns using dark-burned headers.

Flemish bond.

English and Flemish bonds are said to be quarter-bonded because the overlap dimension is half of the width of a header, equivalent to a quarter of the length of a brick.

For structures in which a reduction of strength is acceptable, e.g. in free-standing walls or modest buildings of domestic scale of up to three storeys, the basic bond patterns are often varied to show a greater proportion of stretchers in the face of the wall. This reduces the number of bricks in the face of the wall and, therefore, the cost of thick walling because the majority of bricks are internal, not subject to weathering and therefore they can be of lesser quality. These variants are often referred to as garden wall bonds, but they are frequently used in buildings.

English garden wall bond has courses of headers with from three to seven courses of half-lapped stretchers between them. The photograph on page 76 shows three courses of stretchers and that on page 77 shows an example with six. Common bond, also

known as facing bond, is similar to English garden wall bond with three courses of stretchers between courses of headers, but the stretchers are quarter-bonded not half-lapped. It can be seen in older buildings throughout Britain, but it seems to have been more widely used in the Midlands and northern counties (*see* the photograph on page 78).

Stretcher bond, or stretching bond, is extensively used in modern building because brickwork is normally thin. The outer leaf of cavity walling is only half a brick thick – 102mm (4¼in) – and the bricks are laid end-to-end in courses, each brick lapping over two in the course below.

For simplicity and economy, half-brick walling is normally built with bricks overlapping by half their length. The long faces of the bricks, the stretchers, show in the face of the work. The photographs on pages 71, 73 and 85 show good examples. There are variations in which the overlap is a third or a quarter of the brick length, but these require special cutting

English garden-wall bond.

at the corners and ends of the walling and are not common.

One-brick walls are often built as two stretcher bonded leaves that are tied together. This arrangement is called a collar-jointed wall and the leaves are fixed together with metal ties. Ties can be flat stainless steel ties built in at a similar frequency as ties for a cavity wall. Alternatively, stainless steel wire reinforcement welded in a ladder form and built in across the wall in every third or fourth bed joint is convenient for straight work.

English and Flemish Bonds with Cavity Walling

To match existing brickwork when building new cavity walling, English or Flemish bonds can be replicated in the half-brick outer leaf of the cavity wall by using whole bricks and bats (half bricks, also called 'snap-headers'). The bats should be carefully cut, preferably by a masonry power saw. Either half-

stretcher faces or true headers can be used in the face of the wall. The obvious option is to use the headers, but sometimes they are a slightly different colour and the half stretchers might be a better choice. Also the half stretchers will be slightly wider than the header and this would allow a narrower vertical joints between the bricks – a feature of some older brickwork. When the choice has been made, be consistent in the work.

Although the incorporation of bats in the wall is slightly more expensive than simple stretcher bond, it is not an unreasonable specification where matching an existing bond is important, or where a decorative effect is required.

Decorative Bonds

Brickwork was often used as infill panels between the stud members of traditional hardwood timber-framed buildings. Frequently it was a replacement of wattle and daub infill that had perished, but

English garden wall bond with six courses of stretchers between courses of headers.

Flemish garden wall bond (also known as Sussex bond).

*Common bond
(also known as
facing bond).*

A highly decorative flying bond such as this needs a large plain surface to look well.

sometimes it was the original material. Herringbone bonded work was commonly used for this application.

Decorative bonded patterns are sometimes used as feature panels within plain bonded brickwork (*see* the photograph on page 7). They are usually formed as the half-brick outer leaf of a cavity wall or as a half-brick surface layer of thicker brickwork. In either case, stainless steel wire ties should be used in the joints to secure the panel to the associated backing masonry.

This wall of courses of glazed soldiers and buff headers has an 1920s art deco character.

This decorative free-standing wall has waved courses that incorporate tiles to increase the distortion.

Header bond suits curved work.

Header bond, or heading bond, is used in walls of one brick or more thickness. As the name implies only the ends of bricks are shown in the face of the work. It has a fine, very ordered, appearance and was used for buildings of high quality. Historically it was often built with the grey- or black-coloured ends of bricks that formed the stoke holes in traditional coal- or wood-fired kilns. The bond cannot cope with corners without revealing three-quarter stretcher faces and that is not satisfactory if they are not the same colour as the headers. For this reason, quoins and jambs of openings in header-bonded walling often form features of bonded brickwork of another colour.

Header bond is often used for curved brickwork because the extra joints and short faces produce a smoother curve.

Bonding Bricks

The illustrations of bonding show that specially cut bricks are needed in courses at, or next to, the end of walls and corners in order to bring the pattern to a vertical line. These are known as bonding bricks and are normally cut from standard bricks, as required. The three most commonly used are the half bat (or snap-header), the three-quarter bat and the queen closer, which is a brick cut in half lengthwise, i.e. a quarter brick wide. There is also a king closer, a brick with a corner cut off to leave a half a header and half a stretcher face.

The illustrations of bond types show bonding bricks in plain brickwork, but they are also used when bonding attached and free-standing piers. Examples are shown in the figure on page 81.

FREE-STANDING WALLS

The simplest form of brickwork is a free-standing wall. It may be used to define areas within a site or may form a boundary barrier. Free-standing walls are more expensive than timber fences, but they are more substantial, permanent structures and can be built curved or irregular in plan more easily. Brickwork provides an attractive background for planting and a stable support for climbing plants.

Bonding bricks in use.

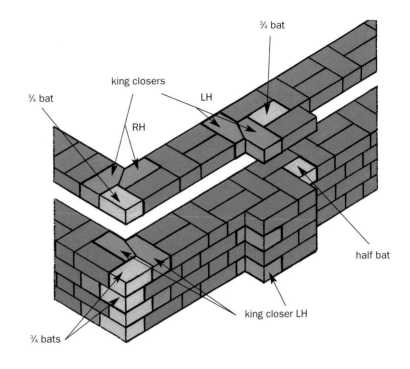

Free-standing walls are simple in concept but they need careful attention to design and specification. It is dangerous to assume that design merely means deciding on the length and height required. It is vital to recognize that free-standing walls are exposed to wind and they are vulnerable to being blown over unless they are properly designed. The collapse of a boundary wall can have lethal consequences and so its stability is of prime importance.

Because they are exposed to the weather on both faces, free-standing walls are liable to get wetter and colder than the external walls of buildings and remain so for long periods. Therefore, durability is a prime consideration.

The relative slenderness of a free-standing wall affects its stability in relation to horizontal forces. A wall of only half-brick thickness has very limited potential and is not considered stable if higher than 725mm (2ft 5in), even in a very sheltered location. For a one-brick thick wall (215mm/9in) in a very sheltered location, the maximum height should not exceed 1925mm (6ft 4in). In a very exposed location, 1075mm (3ft 6in) is the limit for a one-brick thick

wall and one-and-a-half brick thickness (327mm/13in) would be required for 1825mm (6ft 1in).

A very sheltered location is typically one shielded by neighbouring buildings in a town or city, in a region that does not normally experience excessively high winds. In contrast, in regions that are liable to very high winds, locations that have no shelter will be subject to strong horizontal wind forces. Between these two extremes conditions vary considerably. As the dimensions above indicate, designing for a 'worst case scenario' would be uneconomical in most instances, but designing for an average exposure would be dangerous. For sites in the UK, the Building Research Establishment Good Building Guide 14: *Building Simple Plan Brick or Blockwork Free-Standing Walls* provides a rule-of-thumb guide for the design of free-standing boundary walls. It gives maximum height and minimum foundation width for walls of half-brick, one-brick and one-and-a-half-brick thickness in sheltered and exposed locations. As an alternative, a structural engineer would be able to assess the appropriate wind exposure and design a stable wall for a particular site.

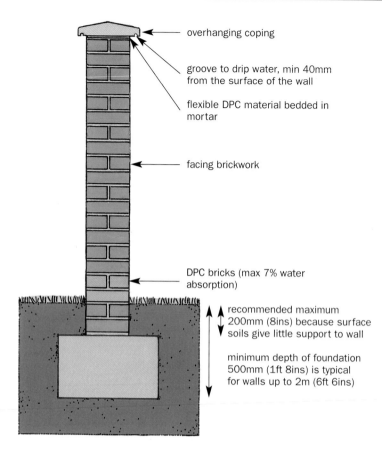

Vertical section through free-standing wall.

overhanging coping

groove to drip water, min 40mm from the surface of the wall

flexible DPC material bedded in mortar

facing brickwork

DPC bricks (max 7% water absorption)

recommended maximum 200mm (8ins) because surface soils give little support to wall

minimum depth of foundation 500mm (1ft 8ins) is typical for walls up to 2m (6ft 6ins)

Piers are recommended to strengthen the ends of walls of half-brick and one-brick thickness as shown in the illustration opposite. The piers would be suitable to support a light gate, e.g. 1200mm high × 800mm wide (48 × 32in) weighing a maximum of 10kg (22lb). Obtain specialist advice if heavier gates are to be supported.

Increasing the thickness of a plain wall will increase its resistance to being blown over, but the plan shape of a straight solid wall is not very efficient, because of its narrow base. Walls of the same thickness, shaped to have a greater effective width, have a greater resistance to horizontal force. Typical shapes are illustrated in the figure on page 84.

The diaphragm wall is a particularly interesting type. As shown in the diagram, on page 84 it appears to be a thick wall, but it is not solid. The cross-ribs (typically at five-stretcher intervals) are bonded into both half-brick leaves so that the whole structure acts

together in resisting wind forces. A wall like the one shown in the diagram on page 84 uses less than 5 per cent more bricks than a one-brick thick solid wall, but can resist wind loads on walls over 2m high (6ft 6in) in most locations. By increasing the overall width of the wall, and hence the length of the ribs, a very strong structure is created. A diaphragm wall of two-brick width overall and 3m (10ft) high is stable in exposed locations. Tall walls of this type of wall are sometimes found enclosing walled gardens of Victorian country houses.

Piers can also be used to stiffen a straight wall, but in a free-standing wall they must project both sides. They are not very effective unless they are quite large. If reinforced by building-in vertical steel rods anchored into the foundations, their efficiency is greatly improved. Half-brick thick walls with reinforced piers 1800mm (6ft) apart can be built up to 2.5 m (8ft) high.

(a) half-brick thick wall in stretcher bond

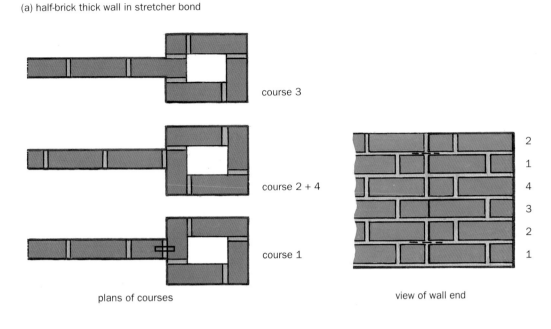

course 3

course 2 + 4

course 1

plans of courses

view of wall end

(b) one-brick thick wall in English garden wall bond

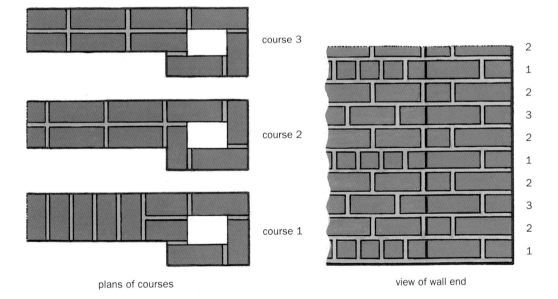

course 3

course 2

course 1

plans of courses

view of wall end

End piers to free-standing walls: (a) half-brick thick wall in stretcher bond; (b) one-brick thick wall in English Garden wall bond.

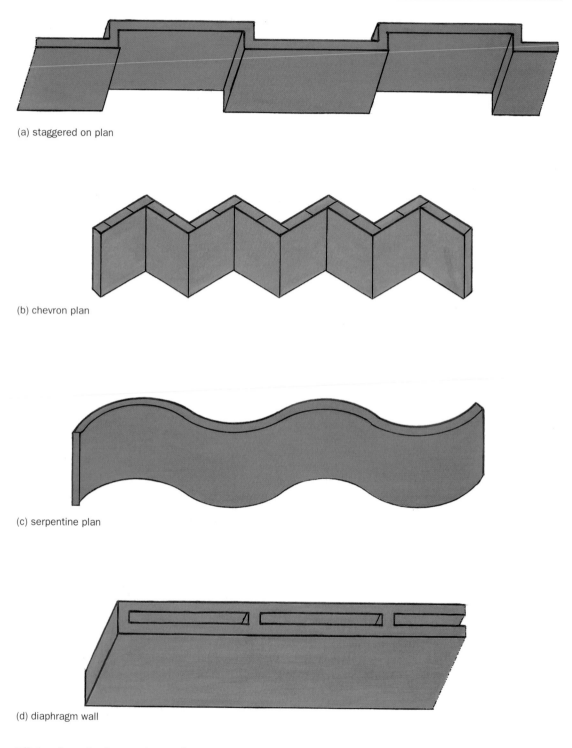

(a) staggered on plan

(b) chevron plan

(c) serpentine plan

(d) diaphragm wall

Efficient forms for free-standing walls.

Staggered plan free-standing wall.

Serpentine free-standing wall.

Piered free-standing wall.

Building Research Establishment Good Building Guide 19: *Building Reinforced, Diaphragm and Wide Plan Free-Standing Walls* provides detailed guidance on the design and construction of these more efficient forms of free-standing walls. Values for wall height, foundation width and diameter of steel reinforcement for piers are given for the various levels of exposure across the UK.

Movement Control

Although masonry seems to be robust and static, it does move very slightly in response to changes in moisture content and temperature. Clay bricks are fired at very high temperature during manufacture and for a number of years afterwards they expand very slightly as moisture from the atmosphere is taken into the molecules of the material. In addition, the brickwork also expands and contracts as its temperature rises and falls in response to environmental changes. The net effect of these movements is a slight expansion over years.

In brickwork of modest dimensions, stress caused by this expansion is accommodated without problems, but brickwork longer than about 12m (40ft) should be interrupted by movement joints. These are vertical joints that are continuous for the full height of the wall. They separate the wall into discontinuous lengths to prevent cumulative stress of expansion that could cause cracking, movement and possible instability. In detached houses, the dimensions of uninterrupted clay brickwork are rarely so large that they require movement joints.

The standard recommendations are that the joints should be located at not more than 6m (20ft) from a corner or end and the distance between them should not exceed 12m (40ft). If there are changes of level in the length of the wall, movement joints can conveniently be located at those positions. Short returns in brickwork can be rigid and if they interrupt long straight runs they can concentrate stress and cause cracking. Treat short returns as corners, even if they are only a half brick offset.

Some brick manufacturers recommend more frequent movement joints in new free-standing walls. This is because free-standing walls have less structural restraint than the walls of buildings because they are not subjected to vertical loading and they have little self weight, particularly if they are low in height. Also they are generally comparatively thin and built with cement-based mortar. Furthermore, some clay bricks have greater potential for moisture expansion than others and although the differences are not great, more frequent movement joints are considered advisable when using them. A manufacturer's advice could be obtained for specific proposals, but as a general guide the following provisions are recommended. When using soft-mud, stock bricks and fletton bricks, the standard guidance can be followed, but when using low water absorption, engineering types of brick, reduce the distance of joints from ends and corners to 4m (13ft) and spacing between joints to 8m (26ft).

Telescopic tie for use in a movement joint in a free-standing or retaining wall.

The joints should be continuous for the full height of the wall including any coping or capping. They should be 15mm (⅝in) wide and filled with a soft, compressible polyethylene or polyurethane cellular foam to keep stones or mortar out and allow the gap to partially close over time. Do not use fibreboard or polystyrene boards, as they are not sufficiently compressible. A flexible sealant may be applied for a neat finish, particularly to the joint through the coping or capping, but the joint must not be pointed with mortar.

To maintain alignment of the wall across a movement joint, slip ties can be incorporated. Space these at third points between ground level and a topmost tie placed in the joint four or five courses below the top of the wall. Slip ties should be of stainless steel, shaped at one end to bond with mortar in a bed-joint on one side of the movement joint. The other end should be plain and enclosed in a plastic sleeve with a gap at the end at least equal to the width of the movement joint; it is set in the corresponding mortar joint in the adjoining length of wall. These ties permit closure of the movement gap, but resist movement in any other direction.

When using calcium silicate and concrete bricks, movement joints need only be 10mm (⅜in) wide, but they should be more frequent. For calcium silicate bricks, place joints no more than 4.5mm (15ft) from ends and corners and not more than 9m (30ft) apart. For concrete bricks, the corresponding figures are 3m and 6m (10ft and 20ft). The length of any panel between movement joints in calcium silicate or concrete bricks should not greater than three times its height, e.g. 5400mm for a 1800mm high wall (18ft for a 6ft high wall). Therefore this requirement, rather than the recommended maximum spacing, will determine movement joint spacing when using these materials in free-standing walls.

RETAINING WALLS

On a sloping site it is often preferable to level some areas and use a retaining wall to support higher ground rather than form a steep bank. If the difference in the ground levels on either side of the base of a boundary wall is greater than twice its thickness, the wall also has a retaining function. Even on level sites, a raised planting bed has to be strong enough to support the soil within it.

A retaining wall.

Retaining walls are designed to resist the horizontal load of the earth that bears on the back of the wall and tends to push it over. The greater the difference in the ground levels, the greater the load will be. Half-brick thick walls are too slender for most applications, as they would only be suitable for a wall about 300mm (12in) high.

Straight, one-brick thick brickwork will be satisfactory for walls up to 825mm (33in) high, but if staggered on plan or piered, the strength is sufficiently enhanced to be stable up to 1575mm (5ft 3in). The illustration on page 88 shows details of these forms of retaining walls.

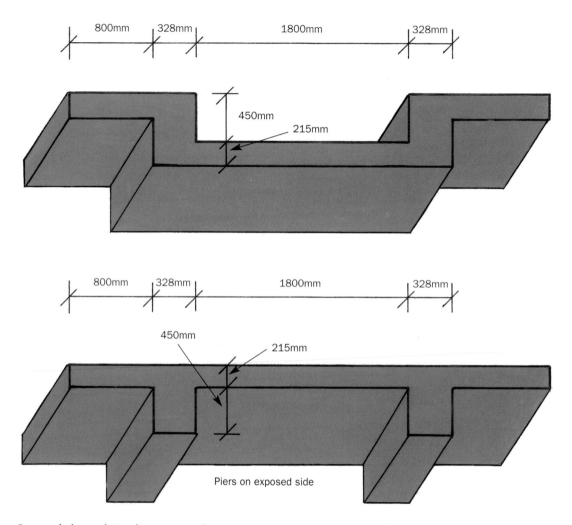

Staggered plan and piered retaining walls to support up to 1575mm (5ft 3in) height of soil.

Retaining walls are exposed to the weather and are also liable to get wet from ground water and remain so for long periods. Durability of the bricks and mortar must be considered with care and design should protect against ground water. The essential points are noted on the illustration on page 89.

Movement joints should be incorporated in retaining walls, but the restraint provided by the retained ground does make them less vulnerable to movement. The standard recommendations set out above, with reference to free-standing walls, should be followed.

If a retaining wall continues up above the upper ground level as a free-standing wall, movement joints should be continuous throughout the overall height.

Further information on the construction of retaining walls is given in Building Research Establishment Good Building Guide GBG27: *Building Brickwork or Blockwork Retaining Walls.* It provides a rule-of-thumb guide for the construction of a range of

Vertical section through a retaining wall.

This shows a wall suitable for a height of 1125mm (3ft 8ins) above the top of the foundation

For heights up to 825mm (2ft 9ins) the wall can be one brick thick throughout its height

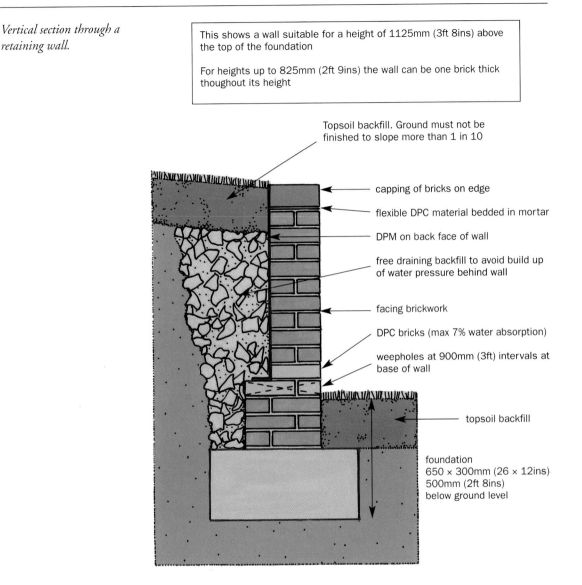

Topsoil backfill. Ground must not be finished to slope more than 1 in 10

capping of bricks on edge

flexible DPC material bedded in mortar

DPM on back face of wall

free draining backfill to avoid build up of water pressure behind wall

facing brickwork

DPC bricks (max 7% water absorption)

weepholes at 900mm (3ft) intervals at base of wall

topsoil backfill

foundation
650 × 300mm (26 × 12ins)
500mm (2ft 8ins)
below ground level

common types of masonry retaining walls up to a height of 1725mm (5ft 9in). It includes straight, staggered, piered and reinforced types.

SOLID EXTERNAL WALLS FOR BUILDINGS

Half-Brick Thick Walls

It is quite common to use half-brick thick walls, without rendering, for domestic garages. They are less robust than one-brick thick or cavity walls, but quite strong enough to carry the loading from a roof above. They have to resist strong winds or other forces that might topple them, but the roof stabilizes the top of the walls and therefore they are less vulnerable than thin free-standing walls. To improve stability, half-brick walls are stiffened by piers or corners at their ends and at intervals of about 2400mm (8ft) in their length. In this form they are stable for a height of about 2400mm (8ft).

Half-brick walls, unless rendered, cannot be relied upon to be proof against penetration by wind driven rain. The general acceptance of half-brick thick walls for garages assumes that in most cases troublesome penetration will be infrequent and unlikely to harm a vehicle that, very often, will be wet when it is brought in. Ventilation should be provided to aid drying within the garage.

However, domestic garages frequently accommodate items other than cars, e.g. freezers, work benches, storage cupboards and racking, and these might be damaged by dampness and the small extra expense of building the walls as cavity walls would be worthwhile.

One-Brick Thick Walls

For a building in the 'very sheltered' category of exposure (typically found within built-up areas of towns and cities), the recommended minimum thickness of brickwork is one-brick thick. For more commonplace exposures, one-and-a-half- and two-brick thick walls are recommended. The requirement of thicker walls is not always appreciated, and some designers are under the false impression that a one-brick wall is universally appropriate – especially those who champion a return to solid wall construction and disapprove of cavity walls.

The thermal resistance of one-brick thick walling is inadequate to meet current building regulations. There are methods of adding thermal insulation to solid walling, but choice is limited and more expensive than with cavity walls.

Insulation can be applied internally by fixing cellular plastic insulation boards or mineral wool slabs to the wall, typically with dabs of tile-fixing adhesive, and lining with foil backed plasterboard with a plaster skimmed finish. The thickness of the insulation and lining would be about 125mm (5in). In the case of an existing building, it is unlikely that the same insulation can be applied to reveals of window and door openings because of the limited space available due to window or door frames. Proprietary composite insulation boards can be used as an alternative lining to save space in these positions. This insulation may not equal that of the general areas, but it will prevent cold surfaces that could present a high risk of condensation. If the inner surfaces of external walls within the depth of timber floor structures are accessible, insulation should be applied to them to avoid a condensation risk.

Insulation boards or slabs can be applied externally, but obviously the attractive appearance of brickwork and its advantages of durability and low maintenance will be sacrificed. The insulation will need protection from weather by rendering or cladding with tile hanging, weather boarding, metal or plastic sheeting, or some other impervious system. The thickness of the insulation and cladding may require some alteration of building details at the heads, jambs and sills of door and window openings and at roof verges and eaves.

CAVITY WALLS FOR BUILDINGS

Cavity walls consist of two leaves of masonry built in parallel with a void between them. The leaves are joined together by wall ties built in at regular intervals. When the outer leaf is of brickwork, it is usually a half-brick thick. The cavity must be a minimum of 50mm (2in) wide. The inner leaf may be of brick or concrete block of 100mm (4in) minimum thickness. To improve thermal insulation performance, lightweight concrete blocks are often used for the inner leaf and its thickness increased to 150mm (6in) or more.

Cavity walls are capable of resisting rain penetration in all exposures to wind-driven rain. It is accepted that some water will inevitably penetrate the outer leaf in prolonged periods of wind-driven rain. Wall ties have drips, corrugations or twists to prevent water tracking across the cavity. The water will run down in the cavity either to drain out at ground level or through weep holes at cavity trays.

Lintels support brickwork over doors and window openings and they should have cavity trays immediately above them. Trays are generally of flexible damp-proof course material stepped a minimum of 150mm down from the inner leaf towards and through the outer leaf of brickwork. Trays should be in one piece if possible, but if joints are unavoidable, they must be made waterproof by lapping and sealing following the DPC manufacturer's specification for sealant or adhesive.

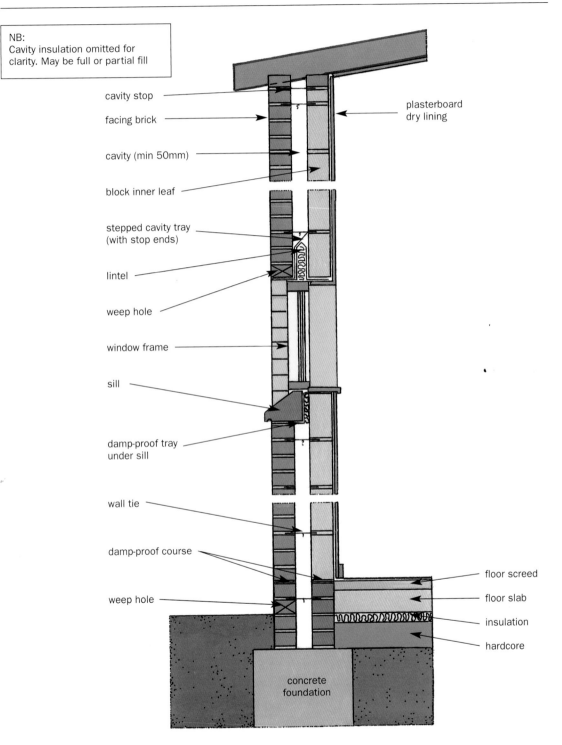

NB:
Cavity insulation omitted for clarity. May be full or partial fill

cavity stop

facing brick

plasterboard dry lining

cavity (min 50mm)

block inner leaf

stepped cavity tray (with stop ends)

lintel

weep hole

window frame

sill

damp-proof tray under sill

wall tie

damp-proof course

floor screed

floor slab

weep hole

insulation

hardcore

concrete foundation

Vertical section through a cavity wall.

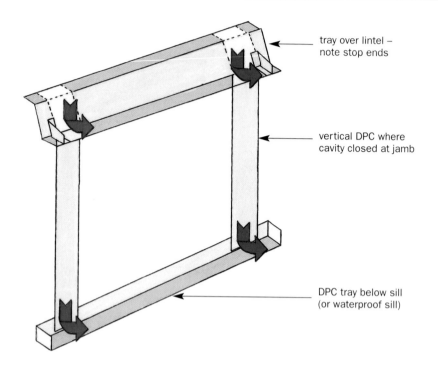

tray over lintel –
note stop ends

*Principle of jamb DPC
and DPC trays above
and below openings
(water is shed to the
outside at laps).*

vertical DPC where
cavity closed at jamb

DPC tray below sill
(or waterproof sill)

The ends of cavity trays must be fitted with stop-ends to prevent water that collects on the tray running off the end into the cavity of the walling below. This is particularly necessary when the cavity contains insulation. Water collected on trays is drained to the exterior through weepholes between bricks at each end; on long trays there should be additional weepholes at four-brick intervals. The figure on page 91 illustrates the main features of a typical cavity wall construction.

Where openings for window and door frames occur in cavity walling, the treatment of the cavity has to be considered. Traditionally, one of the leaves (normally the inner one) is returned to close the cavity and, where it abuts the other leaf, a vertical strip of flexible DPC material is inserted to prevent moisture transfer between the leaves. At the top, the vertical DPC should be lapped behind the cavity tray over the opening; if that is not possible, it should finish tight to the underside of the lintel or be folded back on the inner leaf to hold it firmly in place – it must not be folded forward onto the outer leaf. If there is a cavity tray at sill level, the vertical DPC

should be lapped over rather than behind it. The figure above illustrates these principles.

When the cavity is closed at jambs as described above, the inner and outer leaves of masonry are effectively continuous and heat loss through the solid material is at a greater rate than the general area of the cavity construction. The presence of the vertical DPC, although essential, is negligible in reducing heat transfer. With uninsulated walls, the difference is relatively small, but with the increased thickness of insulation necessary to meet thermal regulations, the difference becomes more significant and leads to greater risk of condensation of moisture on the cold areas of the wall around openings. Therefore in modern cavity insulated walls, some insulation is required in the jamb construction. Various proprietary components, generally referred to as cavity closers, are available. Some are strips of high performance insulation board with DPC material bonded onto them. Others are extruded rigid plastic sections that fit across the end of the cavity between the masonry leaves and act as closers, ties and frame fixings. Some incorporate insulation,

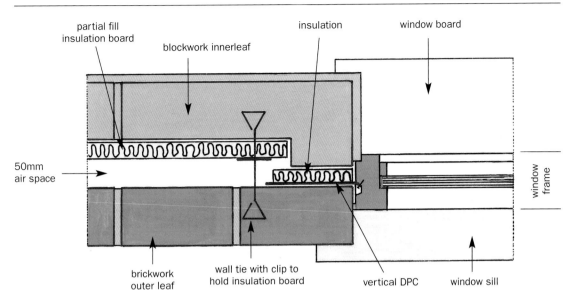

partial fill
insulation board

blockwork innerleaf

insulation

window board

50mm
air space

window
frame

brickwork
outer leaf

wall tie with clip to
hold insulation board

vertical DPC

window sill

Plan of jamb of opening showing insulation.

*Proprietary cavity closer combines functions of vertical DPC, cavity closer, frame fixing and
allows continuity of cavity insulation.*

93

others are shaped to allow the normal cavity insulation to extend up to the back of the window or door frame. Typical designs are shown in the figures on page 93.

Wall Ties

Wall ties connect the two leaves of a cavity wall so that they act together structurally and give mutual support. They are normally spaced 900mm (36in) apart horizontally, in rows 450mm (18in) apart vertically. The ties in successive rows are staggered horizontally. Where the wall comes to a stop, e.g. at jambs of doors and windows and the sloping edge of a gable wall at a roof verge, ties are placed at each blockwork bed-joint position, not more than 225mm (9in) from the edge (*see* the figure below).

Ties should be embedded a minimum of 50mm (2in) in the mortar of bed-joints (not vertical joints) as work proceeds and never pushed in afterwards. Drips to shed water must point down.

British Standard ties are of three types:

- wire butterfly pattern – for cavity widths up to 75mm (3in);
- thick wire double triangle pattern – normal weight for cavity widths up to 90mm (3½in) and heavy weight for widths up to 100mm (4in);
- vertical twist flat bar pattern – for cavity widths up to 300mm (12in).

Ties made from stainless steel are recommended, although galvanized mild steel ties are available.

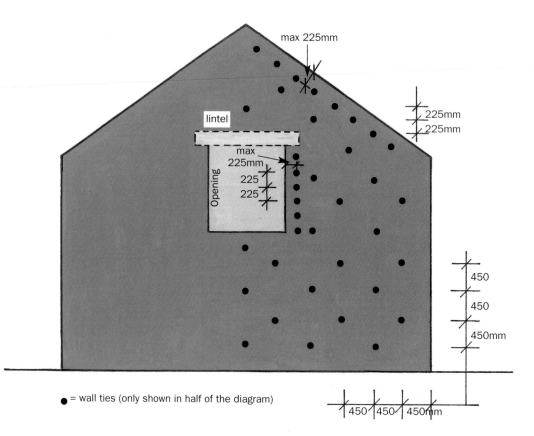

Location and spacing of cavity wall ties.

Proprietary ties are also available, particularly for use with wide cavities that contain cavity insulation. Clips to fit on ties to retain partial fill insulation in position are available. Manufacturers of wall ties and of insulation materials will be able to advise on appropriate ties for particular cavity widths and insulation applications, including clips and supplementary fixings.

Thermal Insulation

For a considerable number of years, insulation has been included in the cavity of the cavity wall to improve thermal insulation. Rigid slabs or boards of insulation can be fixed against either of the masonry leaves to partially fill the cavity, but leaving an airspace of 50mm minimum (2in) (*see* photograph on page 59). To fully fill the cavity, resilient mineral wool batts can be built in as the wall is constructed (*see* photograph on page 58); alternatively, loose mineral wool, polystyrene beads or granules can be blown in when the wall has been built. Properly installed insulation does not reduce the effectiveness of a cavity wall in resisting rain penetration, even in severe exposure conditions. Foamed plastic insulation can be injected as full-fill cavity insulation, but it is not recommended for walls in more exposed locations.

In recent decades, increasing emphasis has been placed on the importance of reducing energy consumption and, in stages, building regulations have required new buildings to be better insulated.

The detailed requirements of the most recent UK Building Regulations that relate to thermal insulation came into force in 2002. Requirements can be relaxed if certain compensatory factors apply but, in essence, the regulations require external walls of houses to have a thermal insulation rating, U-value, of 0.35 W/m^{2}K or lower.

The required rating cannot be met by a wall consisting of a brickwork outer leaf, an empty cavity and an inner masonry leaf, unless the inner leaf is very thick and of very low-density concrete insulating blocks or substantial additional insulation is applied to the interior face of the wall. A wider insulated cavity, of say 75mm or 100mm (3in or 4in), provides an effective and economic construction that can satisfy the thermal requirement with only a small increase in the overall thickness of the wall.

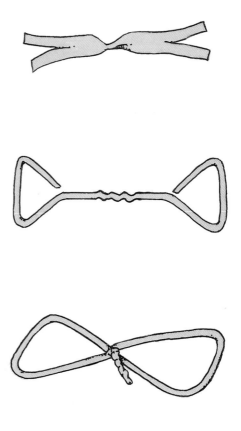

Standard types of wall ties: vertical twist, double triangle and butterfly ties.

Insulation in the cavity and medium-density blocks for the inner leaf have a beneficial effect on the comfort conditions within the building. The thermal capacity of the inner leaf, and any masonry internal compartment walls, helps to stabilize the temperature within the building by absorbing heat to match the internal air temperature. When the temperature drops, it is slowly released again into the rooms. This minimizes fluctuations of internal temperature. The construction also retains the advantages of brick on the external face and of a robust internal surface that will provide support, accept fixings and resist impact damage.

Some modern houses designed with particular attention to energy conservation have brick and block cavity walls with wide cavities filled with

Very wide insulated cavity wall – note long two-part wall ties.

insulation. For example, a wall with a half-brick outer leaf, an inner leaf of 100mm (4in) medium-density concrete block with a finish of 12mm (½in) plaster and a 300mm cavity filled with mineral wool insulation batts has a very low U-value of 0.1 W/m²K. The special wall ties required were a two-part design because in one piece they would be awkward to build in.

Cavity Wall Insulation for Existing Walls

The thermal performance of existing cavity walls can be improved by applying insulation to internal or external surfaces, as described for solid walls, but injecting or blowing insulation material into the cavity is less complicated and the least expensive method. The work requires specialist knowledge and equipment, and therefore should only be carried out by a contractor accredited by a manufacturer of the

insulation material being installed; the installation will then be guaranteed. The installer should inspect the walls and will usually check the cavities to confirm that they are free from debris or blockages. If a barrier is needed to limit the area of cavity fill, e.g. at a party wall line when only one of a semi-detached pair or terrace of houses is being insulated, a nylon bristle barrier, like a continuous giant bottle brush or giant feather boa, is threaded into the cavity.

Foamed plastic insulation is injected into the cavity. Urea formaldehyde (UF) foam is the most commonly used type, but Polyurethane (PUR) foam is also used. Plastic foams are subject to restrictions of their use vis-à-vis severity of exposure to wind-driven rain. The installer should check the exposure rating of the relevant walls to verify the suitability of the proposed insulation material.

Loose insulation materials, such as mineral wool, polystyrene beads or granules, are blown into the cavity. They are widely used and are approved for walls in all categories of exposure.

It is normally more convenient to inject or blow insulation through holes drilled at regular intervals through the external leaf of the cavity wall. Installers are very experienced in drilling the holes and making good afterwards. The work can be done from the inside, but access and disruption of decorations make this a less attractive option.

There are minor differences between the thermal properties of the materials described but, in practice, the improved performance of the wall will be similar, whichever one is used. The limiting factor regarding the potential improvement will be the width of the cavity. In practice, instead of being a nominal 50mm (2in), actual cavity widths are usually about 65mm (2½in). In most houses, when cavity walls are insulated, very worthwhile energy savings are achieved because the total surface area of the walls is normally a very high proportion of the total area of walls, windows and doors.

BRICK CLADDING TO TIMBER FRAMED BUILDINGS

Brickwork is frequently used as a cladding for timber-framed buildings, and in many instances it cannot easily be distinguished from conventional cavity wall construction. The foundation for the brickwork cladding is provided as an extension of the foundation for the timber frame structure. The brickwork is usually a half-brick thick and can be thought of as the outer leaf of a cavity wall, there is a 50mm (2in) airspace and, in place of an inner masonry leaf, is the timber-framed construction. Insulation is located within the timber frame. The airspace behind the brickwork cladding allows ventilation of the timber-frame structure and it must not be obstructed by the addition of insulation.

Wall Ties

The timber frame is self-supporting, but it will benefit from extra support against wind loads from the brick cladding. Flexible stainless steel ties are fixed to the studs of the timber frame with ring-shank nails. Many timber-frame suppliers mark the position of the studs by fixing plastic tapes on the

breather membrane on the surface of the wall panel. If this is not done, similar marks will have to be made on site before cladding is started. Depending on the spacing of the studs, ties should be at every five courses when the studs are at centres of 600mm (2ft) and at every seven courses when they are at 400mm (1ft 4in) centres. In locations exposed to high winds, the designer of the frame may specify a greater density of ties. The top row of ties should have three courses of bricks above and the bottom row should be about four courses above the DPC.

At the jambs of openings and sloping verges, ties should be positioned as described in the figure on page 94, but vertically spaced every fourth course of brickwork.

Differential Vertical Movement

As described when explaining the need for movement joints in free-standing walls, clay brickwork tends to expand slightly over time. On the other hand, timber dries and shrinks if protected from moisture. Therefore, if the timber framing and the brickwork cladding are fastened together inflexibly, with no provision for differential vertical movement, stresses will develop in the system and there will be a high risk of distortion and damage to window frames and at roof eaves and verges.

Window and door frames are normally fixed to the timber-framed structure, projecting from the general plane of the panel to connect with the cladding. They are not fastened to the cladding. Bearing in mind the relative movements of the timber structure (shortening) and the brick cladding (growing), a slight sliding movement will occur at the jambs. The joint between the frame head and lintel over an opening in the brickwork cladding will open, and the one between the frame sill and brickwork below will close. It is vital that there is adequate space allowed below the sill so that the brickwork will not force it upwards. It is recommended that below ground floor windows, 3mm (⅛in) is allowed and below first floor windows, 9mm (⅜in). The gap that opens above a door or window frame should be monitored and sealant applied as necessary.

The differential movement at roof level should be accommodated by allowing a gap between the top of the brickwork and the underside of any roof timber-work that oversails it. A minimum of 6mm (¼in) should be allowed for single storey houses and 12mm (½in) for two storeys.

In detached and semi-detached houses, horizontal dimensions are rarely long enough to require the introduction of movement joints. In the unlikely case of straight runs of continuous clay brickwork exceeding 12m (40ft), vertical movement joints should be introduced, as described earlier in this chapter, under free-standing walls.

Setting Out

Notwithstanding the particular points described above, brickwork cladding to timber-framed houses presents no great difficulties of setting out.

Brickwork cladding should be coursed to the head of openings to achieve correct bearing for lintels carrying the brickwork above them. If a standard door frame is used, its top will normally be 2100mm (7ft) above DPC level on the ground floor, as with masonry walls, and normal 75mm (3in) courses will be used. Panel heights in the ground and upper storey will be the same to maintain consistency of the framing, but the overall thickness of the floor will not necessarily be an increment of 75mm. As a result, the vertical dimension between lintel heights of the two storeys may not be a precise increment of 75mm. Knowing this, a small alteration in the gauge of the brickwork above ground floor openings can be made to compensate. Because the discrepancy can be adjusted over so many courses (about 36), the slight alteration needed is not normally visually significant and causes no difficulty in laying.

The timber-frame structure will be based on a grid of either 400mm or 600mm (1ft 4in or 2ft) to maximize the efficient use of sheathing and lining boards. As this is not directly compatible with the co-ordinating size of brick, there will probably be a need for broken bond as described in Chapter 3.

The Brick Development Association publication Design Note 15: *Brick Cladding to Timber Frame Construction* is recommended for a more thorough coverage of the subject, including details of alternative designs for sills, heads and jambs to window openings and details of arrangements at steps and staggers.

FOUNDATIONS

Only very broad general comments on foundations can be made in this book. Their size and depth will depend on the soil types and ground conditions that apply on particular sites. Except for unusual instances where masonry can be built off bedrock or a system of piles and reinforced concrete ground beams, modern foundations will be of concrete cast *in situ*.

The object of foundations is to spread the load of the masonry onto subsoil material that can support the load and remain stable in all seasons, i.e. at a level not affected by movement due to freezing or moisture changes. Typically a depth of about 1m (3ft 3in) is considered appropriate for the foundations of buildings, perhaps slightly deeper in shrinkable clays. Local Authority Building Inspectors will normally be able to give guidance on the soil types and ground conditions to be expected.

Digging to these depths is normally done with a mechanical digger and in cohesive soils a competent operator can dig accurate straight trenches to the required depth with vertical sides. This allows the excavation to be filled with concrete to form a trench-fill foundation. Notwithstanding the additional concrete used, a trench-fill foundation is quicker and more cost-effective than laying a concrete strip foundation of say 200mm (8in) thickness and building in bricks or blocks up to ground level.

The foundation is normally about 300mm (12in) wider that the wall it is to support. Its top surface must be flat and level, and finished at a height normally allowing two or three brick courses below the intended finished ground level. Stepping may be necessary on sloping sites. If so, the steps in the top surface should be accurately set out to correspond with brick coursing. The wall is normally set out centrally on the foundation.

For free-standing walls and retaining walls, where the effect of settlement is not as serious as it is in buildings, a foundation depth of 500mm (20in) is common. It is preferable, for structural reasons, to minimize the height of brickwork below ground level, therefore the top of the foundation should not be more than two or three courses below the intended finished ground level. Foundations for free-standing walls should not be less than 275mm thick and, in the case of reinforced pier walls, not less than 500mm thick. For foundations of retaining walls, the minimum thickness should be 300mm (12in).

CHAPTER 5

Paving

For centuries bricks have been used as a material for garden paths and paving, their small size making them very useful where a small-scale pattern is needed or where a change of scale is wanted within an overall larger pattern. Being of small units, the surface can be laid to gently rolling levels and also in restricted spaces, both of which would be awkward with larger, slab materials.

Paving materials have to be frost-resistant, hard enough to withstand wear and should not become

Dimensions of commonly available rectangular clay pavers			
Length (mm)	Width (mm)	Thickness (mm)	Notes
215	215	35	Units less than 50mm thick are not suitable for flexible paving.*
215	140	65, 35	
215	65	102, 33 or 35	
215	102.5	65, 50, 30 or 33 or 35	
210	105	65, 50	These 2:1and 3:1 formats are specially intended for flexible paving.*
200	100	65, 50	
200	66	65	
100	100	65	These small-sized units are sometimes referred to as clay cobbles.
75	75	65	
50	50	65	

*Flexible paving is a mortarless form of construction in which pavers are laid close together on a compacted sand bed with the joints between them filled with sand.

Paving at Chelsea Flower Show 2002. (Design: The Garden Design Centre)

slippery in wet conditions. Units are manufactured especially for use as paving and they are called pavers to distinguish them from building bricks. Some building bricks are suitable for paving, but many are not. When building bricks are used in paving they are generally laid on edge with their stretcher faces showing. It would be more economical if the bricks were laid flat with their largest surface showing, but in a building brick the bed face is not a 'finished' surface and frequently it has a frog (a sunken area) or perforations. Pavers are made to be laid flat with their largest face showing.

PAVERS

Pavers have a strong visual affinity with bricks and they are made in a range of sizes. The table on page 100 lists rectangular pavers, which are the normal form, but some manufacturers also produce decorative interlocking shapes.

Special-shaped accessory pavers are produced to form features such as upstand kerbs and drainage channels. Some manufacturers also produce sets of special-shaped pavers to lay together to form decorative features, such as roundels, in a paved surface.

Colour and Texture

Clay pavers are manufactured in a range of attractive colours and textures similar to many bricks, but nuances of colour and texture are less significant in view of the robust service expected of paving. Inevitably, dirt and weathering will tend to mask subtle effects.

Surface texture can vary from the coarse irregular surface of some soft-mud, stock-brick types of paver to the fine, relatively smooth texture of the dense engineering-brick types. Smooth shiny surfaced pavers are not made, as this would present a risk of slipping or skidding, especially in wet conditions. Pavers are made to comply with British Standards and European Standards and there are minimum requirements for skid resistance with which pavers have to comply.

Pavers are generally square edged, although the edges of soft-mud stock pavers might be irregular and softer than those of hard, dense, clay pavers. To

Decorative paving feature at Chelsea Flower Show 2002. (Design: The Garden Design Centre)

soften the edges of the some of their pavers, a few manufacturers tumble, or rumble, them to give an attractive worn appearance that looks well in domestic gardens.

Most pavers are plain-surfaced, but some makers produce them with impressed grid patterns of small squares or diamonds, similar to the patterns of nineteenth-century stable pavers. Another traditional pattern has bold chamfered edges and a false central joint; when laid they give the appearance of small square units in a grid pattern. Other more abstract embossed patterns are available.

Pavers intended for flexible paving may have chamfered edges. They may also be nibbed – have raised bars about 5mm (¼in) wide on their sides and ends – so that when one paver is placed against another a consistent narrow joint is formed between them. Chamfers and nibs aid laying and joint filling. The chamfers also emphasize the joints, increasing the visual impact of the laying pattern.

Standards

British Standard BS 6677: *Clay and Calcium Silicate Pavers for Flexible Pavements* covers the technical specification of clay pavers. The European Standard for these materials will soon be adopted and BS 6677 will be withdrawn in favour of BS EN 1344: *Clay Pavers – Requirements and Test Methods*. The standards determine the use of pavers in public, commercial and industrial applications. Any paver complying with requirements of either standard will be satisfactory for domestic applications.

LAYING PATTERNS

The proportion of length to width of pavers laid on their bed face, i.e. the largest face, is 2:1, whereas that of bricks laid on edge (or pavers of the equivalent size) is 3:1. These proportions must be borne in mind when considering bond pattern. Laying pavers on edge is less economical: 50 per cent more pavers would be required than laying them on their bed faces and, in rigid paving, more mortar will also be required to fill the additional number and greater depth of joints.

There are five basic bond patterns. Variations and mixture of these patterns gives a great variety of choice, and the inclusion of borders and panels separating courses can lead to further enrichment of the surface. Not all paver formats are suitable for all the patterns illustrated.

If both 2:1 and 3:1 proportioned pavers are being considering for use in the same pattern, check that the thickness is the same for both, otherwise there will be considerable difficulties in laying. This does not apply to edging, and indeed the use of brick-on-edge, or even brick-on-end, in such positions is often an advantage as it allows more substantial concrete support backing (haunching) to be placed behind it to assist in restraining the edge of the paved surface.

It is normal to base patterns on whole pavers, cut pavers only being used to fit into edges and the non-regular abutments of paving to walls, etc. If half-pavers are included, some attractive patterns are possible with 2:1 proportioned pavers (*see* figure on page 105).

Running Bond

This pattern has a strong linear quality, and the directional nature of the pattern should be related to the overall design concept. Curves in the line of the paving can be accommodated without difficulty, but both curved and straight lines should be carefully set out and maintained using lines and squares, as appropriate, to achieve consistency. Haphazard deviation will mar the appearance of the paving.

Quarter-, half- and third-lap bonds may be adopted to accentuate the linear character of the pattern. But, with quarter bond, care should be taken if curves are involved, as the overlap is easily lost when 'easing' the pavers around the curve.

Stack Bond

This pattern also has a strong linear character – in this case in two directions – and consistent straight lines and squareness must be maintained for a neat appearance. The pattern cannot follow a curve.

The pattern requires a dimensional consistency that is not characteristic of some clay pavers, particularly those of soft-mud, stock-brick type. Clay pavers of quite rustic character can look well laid in such a pattern in rigid paving with a mortar joint that is slightly wider than normal to allow more tolerance of dimensional variation of the units. With all types of

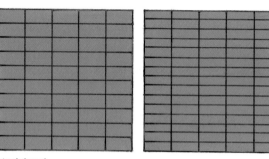

Bond patterns for paving (2:1 and 3:1 proportion pavers) – running, stack, herringbone and basket weave.

running bond

stack bond

herringbone

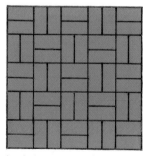

basket weave

Bond patterns using half units
(2:1 proportion pavers).

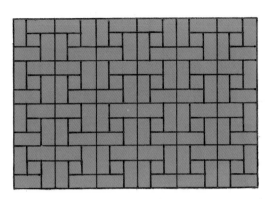

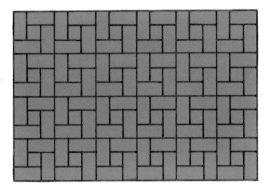

paver, some sorting may be necessary if a precise effect is required.

In flexible paving this pattern presents problems when laying large areas. Because of the minimal joint size, there is limited tolerance of inconsistent size and therefore it is difficult to maintain straightness of continuous joint lines in both directions.

Herringbone

This is a good general-purpose paving pattern without strong directional emphasis, although brick-on-edge versions have slightly more directional quality than when pavers are laid on their bed face. Many designers consider that herringbone patterns tends to enlarge the apparent size of paved areas.

The interrupted straight lines generated by the long edges of the pavers can easily become misaligned, and it is often worthwhile to set out the pattern at 45 degrees to the principal direction of viewing, in order to minimize this becoming notice-

able. However, the disadvantage of doing this is that additional cuts are required for the inevitable triangular edge infill pieces.

This pattern has technical advantages that make it suitable for paving that is subject to frequent and heavy vehicular use. It is appropriate for domestic driveways, but it should not be regarded as the only bond permissible for areas where vehicles have access.

Basket Weave

Although there are straight lines in these patterns, they do have a very static character, and many designers consider that this tends to reduce the apparent size of the paved area. As with the stack bonds, some sorting may be necessary when laying pavers of less consistent shape and size.

Curved and Circular Work

Rectangular pavers laid to curved patterns depend on

Curved pattern paving in rigid paving – the joints allow alignment of the bricks to follow a curve.

the tolerances of the mortar joint to 'ease' the units round the curves. Using cut pavers, more joints are introduced and, therefore, more adjustment is possible. By splaying the cut units, curves to even tighter radii can be laid. Setting out curved patterns calls for skill and care. Special curved units are available from some manufacturers. Also available are special sets of shaped pavers that assemble to form roundels that can be used as a central feature for circular paving.

Curved work is possible with flexible paving, but the minimal joint thickness limits the adjustment of the individual pavers and so only relatively gentle curves are possible.

Although herringbone pattern itself cannot accommodate curves within it, it does relate well to curved or free-form edges and therefore is very satisfactory for curved paths or driveways.

Cutting

Some cutting to complete a pattern or to meet a fixed dimension is generally unavoidable. Cutting at the margins of paving becomes relatively less as the area of paving increases and the shape approaches a square proportion. The implications of designing a pattern that involves abnormal amounts of cutting should not be overlooked – cutting involves extra work and wastage and therefore extra cost.

Pavers can be cut with a bolster and hammer, or with a hydraulic guillotine, but chip-free cuts are not always achieved with these tools. The best method of cutting is with a power circular saw.

ASSOCIATED DESIGN FEATURES

Joint Profile

In rigid paving, the most suitable joint profiles are 'flush' and 'bucket handle'. Flush joints are less suitable for pavers of an irregular shape, or which are unevenly laid. Where arrises are not considered to be vulnerable to damage, a recessed joint can be used to express the individual brick character, although it should be remembered that such joints may impede the flow of surface water and they can accumulate rubbish.

In flexible paving, the joints must always be fully filled with sand. With chamfered-edged pavers the filling should be to the bottom of the V-shaped recess.

Manhole Covers

Manhole covers can disrupt the pattern of paving and need to be located and designed with some care. They should be sited well within an area of paving, aligned with the pattern, and not straddle different finishes, patterns or colours. Existing covers and frames can be taken up and realigned. Metal ones can be painted to tone with the paving. Alternatively, they can be changed for a deeply recessed type in which pavers can be set to match the surrounding surface. Thin pavers may be required, possibly cut specially, and bedded in thin bed adhesive rather than in the normal mortar. Careful setting out is necessary, otherwise the extra effort made to achieve a matching cover will be wasted.

Steps

As a general rule, steps in the open air should be more generous than those within buildings. The dimensions of treads and risers will be dictated by the

Steps formed in paving.

angle of the slope of the ground, unless the whole lie of the land is to be altered. As a guide, the going of the tread should not be less than 300mm (12in), and ideally between 360 and 400mm (14 and 16in). Riser height should be between 100 and 175mm (4 and 7in). It is most important that treads and risers are consistent throughout the flight, irregularities cause stumbling and the risk of falling. To clear surface water, there should be a slight fall on each step, say 6mm (¼in) from riser to nosing – slightly more for very deep treads. Appropriate dimensions can be achieved by using standard format bricks and pavers in a variety of arrangements.

Compared with paving in adjacent areas, a positive change in bond pattern for the treads is advisable as it emphasizes the step edge when approaching the

change of level. This is particularly important when there is only a single step.

Construction consists of a concrete base with paver bricks bedded on it and jointed in mortar. For simple and economical construction, the use of cut pavers, and complicated shaping of the base concrete, should be avoided. This form of construction is vulnerable to lime staining of the steps because rain or groundwater leaches lime from the underlying concrete and deposits it on the surface to form a stain. To minimize the risk of lime staining, the concrete surface should be coated with brush-applied bituminous emulsion damp-proofing material and, while this is still tacky, a dressing of sharp sand should be applied to provide a key for the bedding mortar.

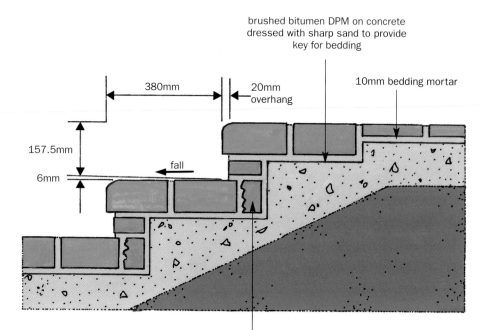

For steps the robust appearance of an on-edge brick as shown is often appreciated

NB Special shape bullnose bricks with small radius bullnose of 25mm are less vulnerable to damage compared with a square edged brick. The large radius 53mm, should be avoided as it tends to impair the definition of the nosing and lead to insecurity.

Vertical section through construction of steps.

DRAINAGE

Paved surfaces should be laid with a fall (a slight slope) to allow rainwater to drain off without causing puddles. Even though the joints in the 'flexible method' of paving described below are sand-filled and not mortared, water will not readily drain through them and the surface must be laid to a fall. A gradient of 1 in 40 is recommended, and 1 in 60 should be regarded as a minimum. Lesser gradients might seem to be acceptable, but they often lead to puddles in wet conditions because of slight irregularities or settlement. In private gardens occasional puddles might seem to be acceptable, but they can cause unsightly staining. Drainage channels, if accurately constructed, may be to a lesser fall (minimum 1 in 100).

In most domestic situations the surfaces of paths, drives and patios can be laid sloping towards adjacent grassed areas or, preferably, planting beds, provided they are relatively free-draining. Where this is not possible, e.g. in a courtyard that s totally paved and enclosed by buildings, or a sunken area surrounded by raised planters, steps up, or other raised edges, the paving should be laid to fall to one or more gulleys that are connected to a soakaway.

Where paving abuts a wall, its surface should be a minimum of 150mm (6in) below the damp-proof

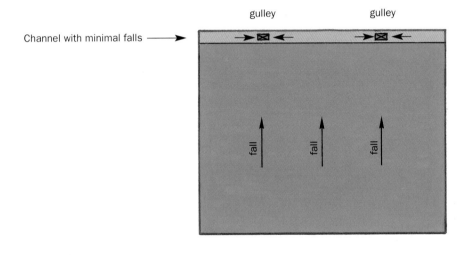

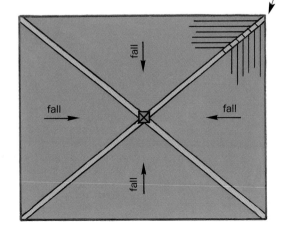

Drainage falls in an enclosed area.

course in the wall. Also, it should be laid to fall away from the wall, so that drained water will not saturate the base of the wall to cause staining and the risk of frost damage. If this is not possible, a drainage channel should be provided at the foot of the wall with a gulley connected to a soakaway. Alternatively, stop the paving short of the wall by about 200mm (8in) and incorporate a gravel filled trench about 150mm (6in) or so deep.

LAYING METHODS FOR PAVING

There are two distinct techniques used for laying pavers – the 'flexible method' and the 'rigid method'. The 'rigid method' is the more traditional one and involves laying a concrete slab foundation and bedding pavers on it in mortar with mortared joints, nominally 10mm (⅜in) wide. The method requires a relatively high level of skill. The laying rate is slow and the work has to be protected from the weather

Rigid paving – a stack bond pattern in which the pavers are slightly twisted to give a scale-like appearance.

Flexible paving.

for several days before use to allow the mortar to set and gain strength.

In contrast, the 'flexible method' of laying pavers is quick: it requires no special skills and the paving can be used immediately it is completed. A stable foundation is required on which the pavers are laid, butt jointed, on a sand bed. No mortar is used. The method is appropriate for the majority of external paving applications and can be successfully done by amateurs. It is not appropriate for internal floors.

The 'Flexible' Method

There are six stages to the construction of an area of flexible paving:

1. Excavating for the construction.
2. Formation of edge restraints.
3. Laying the foundation or sub-base.
4. Preparing the bedding course.
5. Laying the pavers.
6. Compaction and finishing.

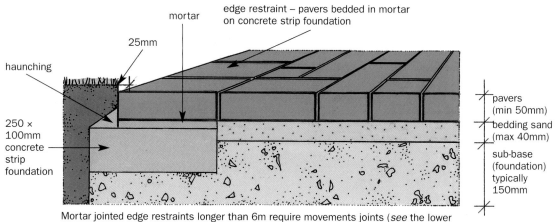

mortar

edge restraint – pavers bedded in mortar
on concrete strip foundation

25mm

haunching

250 ×
100mm
concrete
strip
foundation

pavers
(min 50mm)
bedding sand
(max 40mm)
sub-base
(foundation)
typically
150mm

Mortar jointed edge restraints longer than 6m require movements joints (*see* the lower
diagram on page 118)

Vertical section through construction of flexible paving.

1. Excavate for the Construction

Existing soil, or any other material, must be removed
from the whole area to be paved to a depth to accommodate the construction. Decide what finished level
is required and in which direction the surface should
slope to drain rainwater away.

Excavate at least 225mm (9in) below the finished
level of the paving to allow for the thickness of
construction. If the finished level is to appear flush
with grass, it should be 25mm (1in) below the grass
to allow for convenient mowing without blunting the
mower blades. Use temporary timber pegs and strings
to set out the levels, slopes and edge lines required.
Pegs should be driven-in sufficiently to ensure that
they are firm and not easily displaced during the
work. A straight parallel-edge board and a spirit level
is required for this operation.

2. Forming Edge Restraint

Edge restraint is an essential requirement. It must be
substantial as it is this feature that holds the laid
pavers in place preventing any possibility of horizontal movement, which would open up the joints
and loosen the pavers. Furthermore, and equally as
important, the edge restraint keeps the sand below
the pavers in place; if it flowed out from under the
pavers, they would settle and create depressions.

There are several possible methods of forming the
restraint, the illustrations above and opposite show

typical examples. The base of an existing wall of a
building, or the base of a raised planting bed, can also
fulfil the function. Foundation or haunching
concrete should be kept low to allow for sand
bedding and paving or turf to be laid over it.

3. Laying the Foundation

The foundation, also known as the sub-base, is made
up of freely draining granular material with a
maximum particles size of 75mm (3in) down to fine
grains. This material is known as 'type 1 granular
material' and is used in road construction. It is available through sand and gravel suppliers or builders'
merchants. Do not use rubble or hardcore, as this is
far too coarse and can give rise to settlement
problems.

Alternatively, compacted lean-mix concrete can be
used to form the sub-base. The sub-base material is
placed in the excavation and compacted by a heavy
roller or a vibrating plate compactor. For small areas,
compaction by tamping with the edge of a heavy
board can be satisfactory. The levels and gradients
should be formed in this material so that the next
layer, the bedding course, can be laid evenly over the
whole area.

4. Preparing the Bedding Course

Washed sharp sand (the type used for concreting) is
spread even and level by using a stout, straight-edge

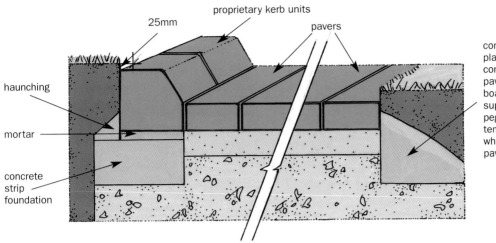

25mm

proprietary kerb units

pavers

concrete bund placed after construction of paving (timber boards supported by pegs used temporarily while laying pavers)

haunching

mortar

concrete strip foundation

Typical alternative edge restraint details.

Spreading and levelling bedding sand (timber boards used as temporary edge restraint and temporary guide for bedding sand thickness).

113

Laying pavers.

board run between temporary battens, the same thickness as the required bedding layer.

To achieve the best regularity in the finished paving surface, the sand should be kept in the same condition throughout the work. Do not let it dry out or become saturated with rain – cover it up between working periods to maintain its condition. Do not use it in a wet state. When laying the bedding course, care taken with consistent compaction and levelling of the surface will make laying the pavers easier and ensure a good finish.

A 40mm (1½in) depth of bedding sand should be laid and well compacted with a vibrating plate compactor; check that the surface is level. When the finished paving is later vibrated there will be a tendency for some of the sand to be forced up into the joints between the pavers from below and the pavers to bed down slightly. So that any such bedding

down will not result in the finished surface being below the edging (slightly above is acceptable), additional sand may need to be added The normal surcharge is 6–9mm (¼–⅜in), depending on the condition of the sand and how effective the compaction of the bedding sand has been.

5. Laying the Pavers

Laying the pavers is quite simple, provided that care is taken with positioning the first few pavers. Bearing in mind the above comments on setting out patterns, set up a straight line to start from with an string line, similarly a second string line at right angles to the first may be necessary to ensure that the pattern is laid square. Each paver should be placed almost in contact with its neighbour. Be careful not to tilt the pavers as you lay them or to knock laid pavers out of place as you proceed, as accidental and unnoticed

Filling-in at edges with cut units. Notice introduction of half-units to avoid the need for small pieces of less than half a paver.

displacements will have a multiplying affect on disrupting the pattern.

The pavers should be laid close together, but not pushed together with any force. A slight gap of about 3mm (⅛in) is ideal. Be sure not to tilt any of the laid pavers by kneeling or standing on them – a spreader board or kneeler pad may help in this respect. Complete the work as far as possible with whole pavers, leaving any cutting at the edges until later.

Surrounding gullies, manholes, etc., may also need cutting and some of these junctions may require the pavers to be bedded in mortar around the fittings.

Treated timber board secured with pegs used as edge restraint.

Plan the work so as to avoid the small infill pieces of less than 50mm (2in). Small gaps of dimensions less than 40mm (1½in) can be filled with 1:3 cement:sand mortar.

Cutting the pavers for finishing the edges can be done with a bolster and club hammer, but for a neater finish – especially if a large amount of cutting is required – an angle-grinding machine with a brick-cutting disc could be used. Such machines can be hired from tool hire shops. Wear goggles and take great care with this work.

6. Consolidation and Finishing
This can be done when a sufficient area has been completed to make consolidation worthwhile. This is usually done with a vibrating plate compactor with a

A vibrating-plate compactor used in laying paving.

rubber-faced plate to avoid chipping and cracking the pavers. If the tool hire company cannot offer you a machine with a rubber-faced plate, then a stout piece of carpet can be roped to the underside of the machine. Without such protection there will be a high risk that the pavers will be damaged.

When laying is complete, guide the vibrator over the entire surface. If only part of the area has been laid, do not vibrate closer than 1m (3ft 3in) from any unrestrained edge. After one pass, dress the surface with fine dry sand, brush it into the joints between the pavers, and make a further two or three passes

with the vibrator. Repeat the sanding and vibrate again. Brush up and remove any surplus sand and the paved area is ready for service.

Some builders' merchants supply kiln-dried sand in bags for this joint-filling operation. Otherwise the bedding sand can be dried and sieved for use; sieving is not essential as the narrow joints will naturally exclude the courser particles and they can be brushed away later.

Check the joints after a week or so, also after rainfall, and brush in more dry sand if the joints are not full. Further vibration should not be necessary.

117

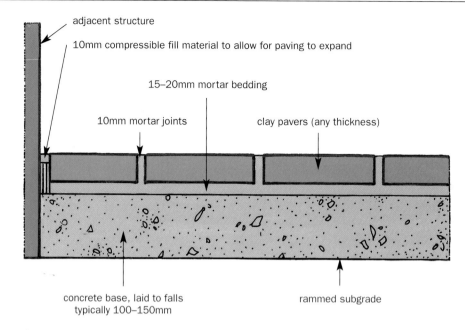

Vertical section through construction of rigid paving.

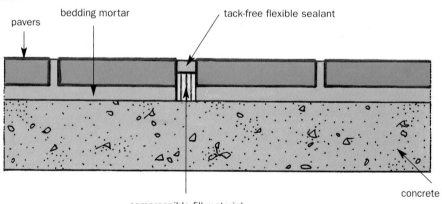

Movement joint in rigid paving.

The 'Rigid' Method

In rigid paving, pavers are bedded in mortar on to a concrete base and the joints between them, nominally 10mm (⅜in) wide, are filled solidly with mortar.

The base may exist or be a new construction. Flexible bases, such as consolidated earth, rolled hoggin or blinded hardcore, should not be used for rigid paving. Generally, the base will be plain or reinforced concrete. Unless ground conditions are unusual, a base of 100–150mm thick (4–6in) concrete, of a compressive strength grade of up to about C20P, would be suitable.

A lean-mix concrete base, typically 300mm thick (12in), could be used for footpaths in vehicle-free areas. Where vehicles have access, the flexible form of construction is preferable. Unless the concrete base is of sufficient strength and thickness, subsequent movement of the ground may result in the slab cracking, which may lead to noticeable cracks in the paved surface.

Where rigid paving abuts existing walls or structures, there should be a compressible joint to allow for the future expansion of the paving in response to moisture and thermal changes. If the dimensions of the paving area exceed 6m (20ft) in length or width, movement control and construction joints in the concrete base will be necessary and guidance for their provision should be sought. Flexible paving does not require such movement joints, except for edging.

The area to be paved should be excavated to the depth required for the proposed construction and the surface well compacted. The levels should be

Rigid paving – this elaborate pattern depends on the bold appearance of the joints.

Bedding rigid paving on a concrete slab.

shaped to suit the proposed finished levels, so as to avoid any unnecessary excess of concrete. Surface falls should not be formed by thickening the bedding mortar. A new concrete base should be well cured (28 days minimum and longer if possible) and may require cleaning before commencing bedding.

Mortars
The mortar used for bedding and jointing of clay rigid paving used externally will be subjected to conditions of severe exposure and therefore good frost-resistance is essential. Generally, only designation (i) mortars (1:3/cement:sand or 1:¼:3/cement: lime:sand) should be used.

Bedding
There are two methods of bedding and jointing pavers with mortar. The preferred method is that in which bedding and joint-filling are carried out as a single operation. The alternative is the so-called 'grouting' or 'tiling' method, in which joint filling is done as a separate operation some 12h or more after bedding. For those inexperienced in the technique, the second method tends to be messy and may result

in the pavers being stained, particularly if they have a rough texture.

In either case, a 15–20mm thick layer of mortar of stiff plastic consistency is spread on the concrete sufficient to enable a reasonable number of pavers to be laid before it starts to stiffen. Mortar should not be used more than 2h after mixing (less in hot weather). It is an advantage to promote adhesion of the pavers to the mortar bed by using a slurry of 1:1/cement:soft sand and water, spread thinly over the bed immediately prior to placing the pavers. Some of the less dense pavers, such as those of a stock-brick character, may need to be dipped briefly in water ('docked' – see page 54) before laying, to reduce their suction and prevent excessive absorption of moisture from the bedding mortar. They should not be soaked.

If, as recommended, bedding and jointing are to be done in one operation, the edge and end of each paver is buttered with mortar and it is pushed into the mortar bed, which has preferably been treated with a cement slurry, as described. Additional mortar, if required, should be carefully placed in the joints by means of a trowel. Any surplus mortar should be

Filling joints in rigid paving with a stiff mortar mix.

removed promptly and a neat profile formed using an appropriate tool.

The surface of the pavers should be wiped clean as the work proceeds, taking care not to smear mortar or slurry on to the surface. Do not leave cleaning until the whole surface has been completed.

With the 'grouting' method, the previously placed pavers are left overnight and mortar of stiff plastic consistency is worked into the joints until flush. A small board of 6mm (¼in) thick plywood approx. 75 × 150mm (3 × 6in) makes an effective tamping tool for joint filling. As before, any surplus mortar should be removed promptly and a neat profile formed using an appropriate tool.

It is sometimes proposed that a dry mortar mix is brushed into the joints and the paving sprayed with water. This is not recommended. Mortar durability will not be as good as when the joint is tooled and it may be reduced further by over-watering. Unsightly cement staining is also likely unless the surplus dry

material is removed very thoroughly and excessive watering is avoided.

Curing Period

The paving must be protected from the weather and traffic while the bedding and jointing mortar sets and gains strength. Cover it with polyethylene sheets against rain, but in hot dry weather the covering should be lifted from time to time and the surface lightly sprayed with water to maintain damp conditions. Pedestrians should not use the paving for four days and vehicles for at least fourteen days.

Cleaning on Completion of Construction

If laying has been carried out carefully, the pavement will be clean and free from stains. However, if the work has been done carelessly, or the pavement is allowed to become saturated soon after laying, cement or lime stains may be present. Such stains may be removed by the use of a dilute hydrochloric

The dark area is of rigid paving forming a feature in a large area of flexible paving in red pavers.

acid solution, using the technique described for brickwork in Chapter 6. Harmless water-soluble efflorescence, which may appear when the pavement dries out completely for the first time after laying, should be allowed to weather away naturally.

MAINTENANCE

Regular brushing by hand is recommended to keep clay paving attractive. Moss, lichens and algae should not grow on clay pavers unless the paving is heavily shaded and damp, e.g. areas under the shade of trees or where drainage provisions are inadequate. If such growths occur, they can be unsightly and slippery. Thick growths should be scraped off and the area

periodically treated with a proprietary moss killer following the manufacturer's instructions.

Weeds and grass can grow in the joints of sand-jointed 'flexible' paving, or in cracks in mortar-jointed paving, although regular foot or vehicular traffic will minimizes this. The growths should not be allowed to become established and mature, as they can disrupt the paved surface. Weeding can be done by hand or by applying a chemical weed killer. Proprietary weed killers that remain persistent for several months, and are specially formulated for use on paving, are widely available.

Cleaning Paving

High-pressure water-jet cleaning is very effective for

Rigid paving – a terrace of square pavers with decorative edging units.

cleaning paving. Pavers are normally robust enough to withstand the abrasive action of the jet. However, mortar joints in paving might be damaged or dislodged by concentrating high-pressure jets on them.

When cleaning flexible paving, to minimize scouring sand from the joints, jets should not be applied at an angle greater than 30 degrees and be directed across the diagonals of the pavers (i.e. not parallel to the joints). When the surface has dried after cleaning, the joints may require some reapplication of sand.

Clay pavers are resistant to permanent staining by oil, but it is unsightly and should be cleaned up as soon as practicable. Absorbent paper or rags should be used to remove liquid oil. Residual deposits can be emulsified by applying degreasing cleaning pastes or liquids, and brushing with hot water or using a steam cleaner. Absorbent paper or rags may be used to mop up the resulting dirty solutions.

The Brick Development Association website provides recommendations for cleaning a variety of stains that may contaminate clay paving. Contact details are listed at the end of this book.

FURTHER INFORMATION

Many manufacturers of clay pavers produce pamphlets describing how to lay their products and some have detailed information on their websites. Advice is also available from the Brick Development Association in Design Notes 8 and 9 dealing with rigid paving and flexible paving, respectively.

CHAPTER 6

Maintenance and Repair

Brickwork's enduring good appearance is one its most valued attributes. If well built it is practically maintenance-free, but after many decades of exposure to weathering there may be some deterioration that requires attention.

Excess wetting of brickwork by water from roof and other surfaces, perhaps due to broken gutters or blocked rainwater pipes, can lead to water penetration, frost damage and problems with soluble salts. The cause of excessive wetting must be corrected before any remedial work to the brickwork is worthwhile.

FROST DAMAGE TO BRICKWORK

The durability of bricks and mortars is explained in Chapter 2. Some are very resistant to damage by frost action and they must be used for brickwork that will be exposed to simultaneous saturation and freezing. Exposure of brickwork to low temperatures is unavoidable, but unless it is saturated, or nearly so, it will be not be vulnerable to frost damage.

Most of the rain driven onto a vertical wall by wind will be rapidly shed. If the mortar joints are finished to provide a good resistance to penetration, wetting will normally be restricted to a few millimetres at the surface of the wall. Saturation is avoided by protecting the top of the wall by roof overhangs or projecting weathered copings and the areas of walling below window openings by projecting sills. Coping or sill units with mortar joints should be set on a DPC to prevent the percolation of water through the joints to wet the brickwork below.

Faulty materials are rarely to blame for frost failure in brickwork. It is more likely to be due to inappropriate specification of materials for rigorous exposure, or the poor design or faulty construction of

Frost-damaged brickwork caused by capping detail not being waterproof.

building details that should have given protection against saturation.

Premature failure of mortar is often due to insufficient cement content. This is often caused by inaccurate measurement of constituents when mixing.

Mortar tends to be less durable than bricks and in older brickwork mortar joints that have deteriorated may no longer provide the resistance to water penetration that they originally did. This may result in increased moisture content in the brickwork and prejudice the durability of the bricks. Repointing, as described later, is the normal remedy.

Frost damage of bricks, referred to as 'spalling', may take the form of a general crumbling or the splitting away of the surface layer.

Surface Treatments

Bricks cannot be treated to improve their inherent frost-resistance. Furthermore, surface treatments that manufacturers claim will protect brickwork from deterioration and improve resistance to weathering can be detrimental to the durability of clay bricks of moderate frost resistance.

Water-Repellent Treatments

Water-repellent materials, frequently silicone-based, are not able to bridge cracks in a surface, even fine ones. Minor cracks are not uncommon in the surface of most brickwork, particularly between brick surfaces and mortar, and so water running down the treated surface could enter the brickwork. Although the treatments are claimed to be 'breathable' and allow wet substrates to dry out, they do seem to inhibit the process and, because of this, saturation levels may be raised and so increase vulnerability to frost damage. From experience, silicone treatments can make clay brickwork, which is exposed to rain, more vulnerable to frost action than it would be in an untreated state.

Paint and Coatings

External brickwork should never be coated with paint, resin-based coatings or sealing materials that claim to be waterproof. Any imperfection in the surface will allow water into the masonry, the coating will prevent evaporation and the moisture will be trapped. As the moisture content increases in the brickwork, so will the risk of sulfate attack and frost action.

Rendering

If frost damage is very extensive and unsightly, brickwork can be rendered. Any loose surface material should be removed to give a firm background. On friable backgrounds, expanded metal lathing can be fixed to give a stable backing. Cement:lime:sand or lime:sand mortars applied in two coats are appropriate. Guidance on the render specification may be obtained from the British Cement Association or natural hydraulic lime specialists (see Useful Contacts). The thickness of the rendering may require some alteration of building details at the heads, jambs and sills of door and window openings, and at roof verges and eaves.

Remedial Work

Minor disfigurement caused by frost action might be acceptable, particularly if remedial work is done to improve protection from wetting and so make further deterioration unlikely. Where damage is considered unsightly, damaged bricks can be replaced, either as whole bricks or as brick slips. Brick slips are 'tiles', about 25 or 30mm thick. They can be supplied by a manufacturer or cut from the face of a brick using a bench-mounted saw (a job best entrusted to a specialist masonry-cutting service).

Finding a supply of bricks to exactly match the originals might be a problem. If there is a redundant brick structure on the premises, the bricks could be reclaimed. A good match is often possible from currently available bricks – seek help from a brick factor or a builders' merchant specializing in supplying bricks. The brick size should also match, but one or two metric-standard bricks isolated in brickwork of Imperial-sized bricks are unlikely to be unsightly. To improve a match, tinting as described later could be used.

Cutting-out and turning bricks to present its other face is sometimes possible, but a trial should be done to establish the acceptability of the hidden face – it may have a very different appearance.

Removing and Replacing Bricks

The removal of single bricks is time-consuming, but

Replacing bricks in an old wall.

can be done using a power drill with a masonry bit. Drill closely spaced holes in the mortar joints all around the brick to a depth equal to the brick width and then break out the mortar with a long thin cold chisel. This should loosen the brick, if the wall is the half-brick thick leaf of a cavity wall. If the brickwork is thicker, a stretcher may have to be prised out after drilling and chiselling out the surrounding joints. Removal of headers in one piece from solid work is more difficult unless the drilling can be done from both sides of the wall, e.g. in a free-standing garden wall. After removal of the first brick subsequent adjacent bricks will be easier to loosen.

Replacing bricks is also slow work. Clean off all the old mortar from the revealed surfaces of the bricks surrounding the void to be filled and, unless they are of low water absorbency, dampen them to reduce their suction. Carefully spread a layer of bedding mortar where the replacement brick is to be laid and press mortar onto the cross-joint surfaces in the wall. Carefully ease a replacement brick into position and press it down onto the bedding mortar – if there is a brick immediately above, the blade of a trowel or bolster can be inserted into the open joint and used to apply the necessary force. Check the alignment of the joints and of the plane of the surface. Allow time for the bed and cross-joint mortar to stiffen and then finish the joints to match the adjoining work. When the mortar is sufficiently stiff to resist disturbance, carefully pack the top bed-joint with mortar. A pointing trowel (smaller than a normal one) will be easier to handle for this task. When that mortar has stiffened finish the joint as before.

If the work is being carried out to the outer leaf of a cavity wall, care is needed to minimize debris or new mortar falling into the cavity. Also avoid mortar being squeezed into the cavity to form ledges. For

Using brick slips to replace damaged brick faces.

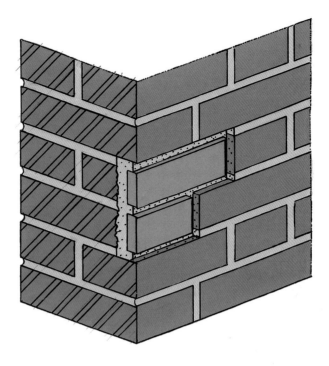

this reason it is a good idea to confine the bedding and cross-joint mortar placed to receive replacement bricks to the front three-quarters of the joints. Mortar squeeze will substantially fill the rear part of the joints but, not being completely full is better than large mortar extrusions into the cavity.

Using Brick Slips for Replacement

As an alternative to the removal and replacement of whole bricks, the use of brick slips is satisfactory for isolated, or a small number of bricks, provided that the cut-back surfaces are sound enough to provide a firm background for fixing.

The damaged surface and adjoining mortar need only be cut back to a depth of about 35 or 40mm (about 1½in), to allow for the brick slip and 10mm (⅜in) mortar behind to fix it. This thickness of new material will provide good protection against further frost damage to the material behind it.

Cutting back can be done with a sharp cold chisel and club hammer. As with removing bricks, the use of a power drill can be helpful and the multiple drilling need not be confined to the mortar joints. Manufacturers of some heavy duty drills offer special masonry routing bits as accessories. An advantage of power drills is that vibration is less harsh than with heavy blows of a hammer and chisel and therefore there is less risk of loosening adjacent work.

When the excavation is complete, clear out loose material and dampen the surfaces of the cavity and the brick slip to reduce suction. Apply mortar at the back of the cavity and carefully press the slip into position, taking care to align the joints and the plane of the surface. Small wood wedges might be necessary to prevent the slip creeping down and out of alignment before the mortar sets. Mortar should squeeze into the surrounding joints, but should be removed within 12mm (½in) of the surface. When the backing mortar has set sufficiently to fix the slip, remove any wedges and point the joints with mortar and finish to match the existing work.

The resurfacing of brickwork using slips in this manner is not recommended for areas larger than about twelve bricks. Larger areas require special provisions for tying back to ensure stability, e.g. stainless steel wire ties set with resin into the backing and/or the use of mortar specially modified to enhance adhesion.

Repointing Mortar Joints

Mortar that is properly specified, mixed and applied, can remain in good serviceable condition for very many decades. A poor mortar may only survive for one or two winters before it fails. After many years of weathering, some deterioration of mortar joints might be apparent and repointing may be needed, but it is never justifiable to repoint solely on the basis of age. If repointing is tackled prematurely, besides being an unnecessary waste of effort and money, cutting out of old mortar will be difficult and the edges (arrises) of the bricks could easily be damaged.

Frost damage to mortar causes it to crumble and disintegrate; in this state it can be eroded and may be lost from the joint. It also becomes very water absorbent and encourages rainwater into the brickwork, increasing water content, placing the bricks at greater risk of frost damage and making the brickwork less resistant to rain penetration.

When mortar failure has been caused by some faulty building detail, or by excess water from an exceptional source, that should be corrected before repointing is commenced. If it is intended to clean the brickwork, that should be done before repointing is undertaken.

The appropriate mortar mix for the repointing should be chosen with regard to the type of brick and the exposure of the brickwork. Except for cappings, copings and sills, where the superior durability of 1:¼:3 mortar is required, strong, cement-rich mortars should be avoided for repointing. They tend to shrink and crack, leading to poor bonding with the brick and cracking at the brick/mortar interface. These factors encourage water penetration and increase saturation of adjacent bricks.

Cement:lime:sand mortars are recommended for repointing because the lime produces good bonding characteristics. In normal exposure conditions for external walling between ground level and roof eaves, a 1:1:6 mix will be suitable for the majority of bricks. For soft, very porous bricks a weaker 1:2:9 mortar would be preferable, but as this mix is particularly vulnerable to frost until it has set and gained full strength, it should only be applied in the summer months.

For repointing other brickwork features, follow the advice given in the table on page 33 for the appropriate mortar mix.

As well as choosing the mortar mix for its technical properties, colour is important, particularly if not all the brickwork is being repointed and a close match of new with old is required. The importance of mortar colour is discussed on page 70. Choose supplies of sand, lime and cement with care to

---

Natural Hydraulic Lime Mortar

Prior to the twentieth century, brickwork was laid in hydraulic lime mortar, i.e. without Portland cement. Hydraulic lime sets by chemical reaction with water and forms a bond with sand and masonry. Pure limes are non-hydraulic and do not have this ability. In some regions, locally produced limes were unable to provide mortar of sufficient strength of bond and durability, and pozzolanic mineral materials were added to give the mortar these properties. In many instances, old brickwork, particularly if the bricks are of medium or high strength, can be repointed with the Portland cement mortars described above. In historic buildings and old brickwork with low strength, porous bricks that may be friable in character, repointing with natural hydraulic lime mortar would be advisable.

For many years natural hydraulic lime was not easy to get in the UK and supplies were imported from the Continent for restoration and repair of old brick and stone masonry. This situation has changed in recent years and natural hydraulic lime is now more readily available. Suppliers are also able to provide information on appropriate mortar mix recipes and the working procedures for its use.

It is most important to understand that natural hydraulic lime cannot be applied on the assumption that is it a simple substitute for Portland cement. Lime mortars set and gain strength at a much slower rate than Portland cement mortars, especially at low temperature. Laying bricks or repointing with hydraulic lime mortars should not be carried out in cold or wet weather.

achieve the desired colour of mortar, and keep them consistent throughout the work. Adding a colour pigment may be appropriate (see comments about using pigments on page 34). Even though it takes time, before embarking on repointing brickwork in a prominent position, it is worthwhile making trials with small sample quantities to determine the correct mix colour.

When only a part of the brickwork is to be repointed, match the original joint profile, otherwise the appearance of the original and repointed areas will not match. If all the brickwork is to be pointed, and the condition of the bricks is good, the profile of the original joint can be repeated. If the finish of the joint is open to choice, consider the use of either a 'bucket handle' or 'struck weathered' profile, as these are neat and easy to form and they perform well, minimizing water penetration of the joints. Never finish the joints proud of the edges of the bricks. Mortar should not extend over onto the brick face – besides looking ugly, the thin section will shrink, crack and encourage rainwater behind it and into the joint.

Repointing Procedure

Repointing should not be undertaken in winter because the risk of frost and wet weather are unavoidable. This is not only because of the difficulty of providing adequate protection, but also because mortar applied to very cold brickwork sets and gains strength slowly and adhesion can be poor. As noted on page 34, anti-freeze additives are not recommended for used with mortars.

In preparation for repointing, the old mortar should be raked or cut out completely to give a square recess 15mm (⅝in) deep (10mm minimum and 20mm maximum/⅜ and ¾in). The brick edges should be free of old mortar to provide a good bond for the new. This work is best done by hand using a narrow (about 8mm/¼in wide) plugging chisel and a club hammer. With these tools, the cutting can be confined to the mortar without damaging the bricks. Power tools tend to be much less controllable and there is a tendency for the edges of the bricks to be cut and the joints to be widened. As a result, the repointing will look coarser than the original jointing.

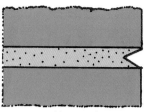

incorrect raking out for pointing

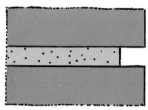

correct deep square key for pointing

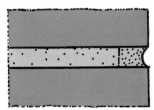

recommended joint profile for good weather resistance

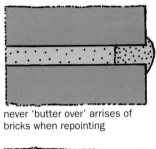

never 'butter over' arrises of bricks when repointing

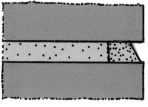

recommended joint profile for good weather resistance

Do's and don'ts of repointing.

Hard dense cement/sand mortar repointing, poorly applied has trapped water behind it and caused frost damage to the brickwork.

When the joints have been cut out, all loose material should be brushed out of the joints and off the surface. The brickwork should be rinsed with clean water to remove dust. Do not use a powerful hose, as this will lead to excessive wetting.

Start at the top left-hand corner of the area to be repointed and work across and then down, completing about two square metres at a time.

If the bricks are of very low water absorption, e.g. similar to engineering bricks, the brickwork should

Using an angle grinder to remove old mortar is not recommended as the tool inevitably cuts the edges of the bricks and widens the joints.

be dry when repointing. If the bricks are of moderate or high water absorption the brickwork should be moistened to reduce its suction so that the water in the mortar is not immediately drawn out of it leaving insufficient for the cement to hydrate and set properly. Moistening is best done using an old flat distemper brush to apply clean water to the raked-out joints. The brickwork must not be soaked, as over-wetting will encourage smearing of mortar on the surface of the bricks.

Prepare a small quantity of mortar at a time, sufficient for about 1–1½ hours' work. Place a small amount on a hawk (a small hand held board) and, using the edge of a small pointing trowel, take some and press it firmly into the vertical joints, the cross-joints, allowing some to squeeze into the bed joints above and below. When a number of cross-joints have been filled, and while the mortar is still fluid, fill the bed-joints using a larger pointing trowel.

An alternative to the use of pointing trowels to fill the joints is to use a skeleton gun and refillable cartridge – similar to the tool used to apply flexible sealants around window frames or bath rims. Conventional cement:lime:sand mortar can be applied in this way, but it should be pushed through a sieve to remove small lumps and stones that might obstruct the cartridge nozzle; a gardening sieve with a 6mm (¼in) mesh is suitable.

Continue filling the joints. Check the state of mortar in joints laid earlier from time to time; when it has begun to stiffen and set, but is still malleable, it is ready for finishing. With an appropriate tool, form the required joint profile (*see* pages 44–5). Take care not to smear mortar on to the surface of the bricks. Remove all loose mortar 'crumbs' from the surface by light brushing with a soft bristle brush. Brushing should not leave marks on the mortar. If there is a tendency for this to happen, brushing is either too hard or being done too soon.

In hot dry weather, and for any work in full sun or exposed to drying winds, newly repointed brickwork should be protected from drying out prematurely.

Pointing joints with mortar using a 'gun'.

Tooling joints to form a bucket-handle profile.

For a few days it should be kept draped with damp hessian that is sprayed with water from time to time. The hessian should be held off the surface of the brickwork by battens to avoid risk of stains caused by smearing the new mortar.

WATER-PENETRATION PROBLEMS

Traditionally, solid brick walls of single or one-and-a-half-brick thickness (225 and 340mm/9 and 13½in) were considered sufficiently rain-resistant in many areas of the UK, particularly within towns and villages. In coastal or other severely exposed areas, brick walls are often rendered or tile hung for additional protection.

A cavity wall offers protection against rain penetration. The design accepts that the brickwork outer leaf is not waterproof and the cavity interrupts the passage of any water, conducting it out again by means of cavity trays and weepholes. The mortar joints are the most important factor in limiting water penetration through a brick wall. All joints should be solidly filled with mortar, particularly the vertical cross-joints (perpends). If they are only partially filled, they offer little resistance to the passage of wind driven rain.

Tooled joint profiles (e.g. 'bucket-handle' or 'struck-weathered') compact the surface of the mortar and help to seal the brick/mortar interface. They keep the water on the surface of the wall and are more effective in resisting rain penetration than a flush joint. A recessed joint profile is particularly vulnerable to water penetration.

The lime in cement:lime:sand mortars promotes good bonding, which benefits the performance with respect to resisting rain penetration.

The density of the bricks in the wall is of no significance in preventing water penetration. Porous bricks absorb water driven onto the wall and hold it temporarily until it evaporates and dries off. Dense bricks, by contrast, absorb very little water and so it flows down the surface of the wall. Defects in the jointing may be subjected to high volumes of water which might then be conducted through them. In protracted periods of wind-driven rain, solid brick walling may become sufficiently wet for the internal surface to become damp.

Brickwork walls of half-brick thickness (102mm/ 4½in) should not be expected to resist penetration by persistent wind-riven rain (*see* page 90). Fully filled cross-joints (vertical joints) minimize rain penetration, and bricks with a high water absorption will beneficially absorb rain and delay penetration – possibly long enough for the rain to stop and the wind to dry the walling.

Where rain penetration is a problem, the mortar joints should be carefully inspected, paying particular attention to the solid filling of cross-joints. Repointing may improve resistance to rain penetration, especially if a tooled joint profile is used as

noted above. Poor cross-joints may also be accessed from the internal wall face.

Surface treatment with sealants or silicone fluids is rarely an effective cure for water penetration and sometimes their use can make the problem worse. A silicone treatment may cause water to run on the surface of a material rather than soak into it, but it is not able to bridge or fill any cracks even very small ones. As a consequence, the flow of water over the surface will subject any cracks to greater quantities of water that will be able to penetrate in these positions. Similarly, if a faulty building detail is the cause of water penetration, surface treatment of the associated brickwork is most unlikely to effect a cure and may increase the quantity of water reaching the defective detail.

Dampness is sometimes experienced at the internal reveals of window and door openings. Often this is not caused by rain penetration but by the

Wind-driven rain can easily penetrate poorly filled joints, especially cross-joints. Leaving joints 'as laid without tooling' also gives poor resistance to rain penetration.

Efflorescence of soluble salts can look unsightly, but it is harmless and temporary.

condensation of moisture from the warmer internal air on the cold surface of the reveal. Internal reveals of openings can be lined with insulation materials, but it is often difficult to do in an existing building because of limited dimensions. Condensation can be minimized by improving ventilation. Avoid restricting air movement and trapping air with bunched curtains at reveals.

Water penetration can occur around window and door frames. Check externally for the presence and condition of sealants and/or cover strips where the window or door frame abuts the masonry and renew or make good as necessary.

Chapter 4 describes cavity wall construction and the installation of damp-proof courses, trays and weepholes. If the rain penetration suggests that there is a fault with the construction, e.g. substantial wetness of internal walling at the sides of openings, it would be best to employ an experienced builder to

investigate and remedy defects. Flexible DPC material can be awkward to manipulate and is easily damaged. It is possible that the remedial work would not be straightforward and may require the removal and refitting of the window frame.

DISFIGUREMENT AND DAMAGE BY SOLUBLE SALTS

Efflorescence

The clays from which bricks are made frequently contain soluble salts. Clay preparation during manufacture and firing processes may remove or reduce them, although some fuels used in firing may add some. If brickwork is exposed to the weather and rainwater is able to percolate through it, soluble salts will be dissolved and carried in solution to the surface of the brickwork where, when the water evaporates they will be left as a fine loose powder (commonly

Efflorescence removed by natural weathering (photograph taken six weeks later than the one opposite).

white). This is known as efflorescence. It may be a light widespread dusting, patches of whiteness on the surface of bricks or mortar joints, or a heavy and extensive overall deposit.

Regardless of its unsightly appearance it is harmless and provided the surface is exposed to weather it is preferable to leave it to be washed away by normal rainfall. Brushing off dry efflorescence with a soft bristle or nylon brush and a dustpan may accelerate its removal, but even heavy deposits will generally be washed away in a few weeks. Hosing the brickwork will not generally replicate the action of rain. It may initially appear to have worked, but it tends to wet the brickwork too much and, as it dries, efflorescence returns. Chemical cleaning is not recommended.

Efflorescence that occurs on brickwork that is sheltered from rain can be removed by dry brushing, as already described, followed by sponging the surface with clean water. Take care not to wet the brickwork to any depth. Two or three light sponging sessions, allowing the surface to dry between each, will be more effective than a single heavy handed one.

Efflorescence is harmless and temporary, but if the surface is coated with a material which traps the salts behind it, e.g. paint and water resistant coatings, damage may occur due to a build-up of salts behind the coating that forces it off.

Cryptoflorescence

Before the development of inexpensive concrete blocks in the middle of the twentieth century, millions of bricks were required for use internally where they would never be subjected to weathering and great strength was rarely needed. To keep the cost of these internal-quality bricks down, they were not fired as thoroughly as the external-quality ones.

Underfired, internal-quality bricks made with some clays can be vulnerable to damage if they are subjected to damp conditions. The moisture may cause migration of soluble salts to a position just below the surface of a brick causing it to crumble or flake off. This phenomenon, known as cryptoflorescence, is comparatively rare. Examples of locations in which it might occur are in brickwork forming the separating walls between roof spaces of terraced houses, particularly where they continue above the roof as parapet walls, and in damp cellars.

The parapet structure may allow damp penetration below roof level. In a well-ventilated roof space it may dry out without any harmful effect, but cryptoflorescence might occur. If it is evident, check the condition of the brickwork above and repair and repoint the mortar joints and flashings, if they have deteriorated. Brush off loose material from the brickwork surface within the roof space and remove it from the roof. Allow the brickwork to dry. This action may arrest further deterioration, as long at the external repairs remain effective. The loss of up to 12mm (½in) from the surface of a brick would not cause instability. If extensive damage is evident, the masonry may need to be replaced, but the location of the work would present difficulties.

Gypsum Salts

Another unusual cause of surface damage due to salts concerns air pollution and brickwork with limestone masonry features. Before the introduction of Clean Air Acts and smokeless fuels in the 1960s, atmospheres in large towns and cities in Britain were frequently heavily polluted because of the widespread use of coal fires for heating. In these atmospheres and damp conditions, limestone forms gypsum, which is dissolved by rain and may be washed down into the surface of any brickwork below. Here, the gypsum

Surface damage of soft red bricks by gypsum salts.

*Sulfate attack to
brickwork
behind rendering.*

crystallizes and expands, and may cause surface damage to porous bricks. This type of damage is not very common but can be the explanation of puzzling surface deterioration that is similar in appearance to frost action, but occurs below what seem to be protective stone copings, sills or decorative features.

Cleaning of the affected areas will generally stop further deterioration, as environmental controls now eliminate the pollution levels formerly experienced. Roughness of a damaged, formerly smooth, surface can be reduced by rubbing with a flat carborundum or grit stone.

Sulfate Attack of Mortar

If brickwork of clay bricks that contain soluble sulfates is wet for long periods the sulfates can cause a damaging expansive reaction in the mortar. This is not a commonplace defect, but there are some structures that are particularly liable to substantial wetting and therefore are at risk. The top metre (3ft) or so of free-standing walls with brick-on-edge cappings usually get very wet in rainy weather and remain so for a long time. Earth-retaining walls also get wet and, if there is no vertical damp-proof membrane to stop water entering the brickwork from the higher ground behind the wall, that will increase moisture content.

The classic appearance of sulfate attack in brickwork mortar is a crack in the centre of each of the bed-joints (*see* figures on pages 28 and 32). If the mortar is very weak, it quickly disintegrates and crumbles with no dominant crack. Sulfate attack is not confined to the surface of the mortar and affects the whole joint. Repointing is not an effective treatment. Ultimately, the affected brickwork loses stability and should be demolished and rebuilt. The bricks can be reused with a more durable mortar specification as noted on page 33.

Sulfate attack can sometimes occur in rendered brickwork. Fine horizontal cracks spaced at 75mm (3in) in cement and sand rendering signify that water has penetrated the render, built up moisture levels in the brickwork beyond and caused sulfate attack in its mortar joints. Replacing the rendering is not an adequate remedy. The brickwork should be rebuilt with mortar resistant to sulfate attack. The building details should also be improved to minimize water getting behind the rendering. Rendering should not be applied to both sides of a clay brick freestanding or parapet wall.

LIME STAINING

Lime staining in the form of a white bloom or bleeding is commonly the result of the excessive wetting of brickwork by rainwater during its early life. All masonry is vulnerable, but brickwork built of low water-absorption bricks is particularly so.

New mortar made with Portland cement, although set and gaining strength, contains a water soluble form of lime, calcium hydroxide (sometimes called 'free lime'), which is produced as the cement sets. Unless the top of masonry under construction, or newly completed, is protected by temporary covering, rainwater can enter the mortar and dissolve the calcium hydroxide. The solution passes out, particularly if the bricks do not absorb much water, and onto the wall surface where the dissolved material is deposited as the water evaporates. Although soluble, the deposited calcium hydroxide quickly reacts with carbon dioxide in the air to form calcium carbonate, which is not soluble and will not wash off easily.

The insoluble lime deposit can be in the form of a film of whiteness or as streaks, often concentrated below the vertical cross-joints in the brickwork. Light general 'blooming' may weather away in well-exposed walls, but this might take a long time. Concentrations in the form of streaks are unlikely to weather off and should be removed. An effective method is described below.

As mortar matures and air penetrates it, the carbonation of its soluble lime content occurs within the mortar and, therefore, lime bloom or staining does not re-occur in normal brick walling.

In large concrete elements, e.g. reinforced slabs, beams and paving units, the carbonation of 'free lime' takes much longer than it does in mortar because there is a greater cement content and air penetration is restricted by the denser material. Design detail should prevent the passage of water through concrete and onto the surface of any associated brickwork, otherwise the concrete could be the source of lime

Lime staining from mortar joints.

Lime staining from rain percolating through concrete slab paving of the raised terrace.

staining for some considerable time. To minimize risk of lime staining, newly cast concrete or reconstructed stone cappings and sills should be left covered, but well-aired, for some weeks before fixing.

In hard water districts, lime staining can be seen on surfaces wetted by persistent overflows from water storage tanks or WC cisterns.

Acid Cleaning to Remove Lime Stains

Lime staining can be removed from brickwork surfaces by careful cleaning with dilute hydrochloric acid, also known as 'spirits of salts', or a proprietary brickwork cleaner based on it. A solution of 5 per cent is normally effective, but for stubborn stains up to a maximum of 10 per cent can be used. This treatment is also used to remove mortar stains from the face of bricks.

The cleaning may be undertaken by a specialist contractor but, provided that appropriate health and safety requirements are observed, the work is within the capabilities of the average handyman or woman. Protective clothing should be worn, including waterproof gloves, footwear and eye protection. If acid is splashed on to skin, it must be washed off immediately with clean, cold water. A solution of bicarbonate of soda (baking soda) should be at hand as a first-aid precaution in case the acid is accidentally splashed on to the face.

The surface to be cleaned must first be well wetted with clean water to kill the suction, thereby keeping the reaction at the surface and preventing the acid being drawn into the masonry. Unless it can be protected by effective covering, walling below the area to be treated should also be wetted to prevent contamination by the rinse water. Rinse the whole area with clean water on completion of the treatment.

Cleaning should be tackled in small areas, as the acid should only be in contact with the brickwork for a very short time (seconds not minutes) and then be rinsed off with clean water.

An effective procedure is to have to hand a hose with a modest flow of clean water, a container of acid cleaning solution and a paint brush (say 50–70mm/2–3in wide). With the brush, apply the cleaning solution to staining on a brick face or mortar joint (a fizzing reaction should start immediately and then subside), rinse off with water from the hose and repeat as necessary until the stain is removed. Some agitation with the brush will assist.

Efflorescence may be induced by the wetting required in this procedure. See notes above regarding its removal.

Selective rebuilding is the most practical remedy for some cracked and distorted brickwork.

STAINING BY VEGETATION

Various forms of vegetation, like moss, algae, fungi and moulds, can grow on moist brickwork causing green, brown or black coloration, but it is not likely to become very noticeable unless the brickwork is wet for long periods. Even so, if it is uniformly distributed rather than concentrated in streaks or patches, it may not be considered unattractive. For example, darkening of capping bricks on a garden wall, or a light growth of moss, may be considered an attractive sign of ageing, but dark or green streaks that follow the flow pattern of water down from the top of a wall, or from the ends of a window sill, are generally unsightly.

To remove this form of staining, first scrape off as much of the plant material as possible with a wooden or plastic scraper or a stiff bristle brush. Small quantities of dissolved copper salts have a very toxic effect on moss, moulds and fungi. An effective control measure is to apply a wash of 30g (1 ounce) of copper carbonate dissolved in 4.5ltr (1 gallon) of water with a little household ammonia. Copper sulfate solutions should not be used on masonry.

CRACKS AND INSTABILITY

The need to identify and remedy the cause of cracking is essential before any repair of the damage is worthwhile. It is beyond the scope of this book to discuss in detail the various factors that may lead to cracking in brickwork, but it may be due to one or more of the following:

- movement or failure of ground support or foundation (i.e. subsidence);
- structural failure of wall or associated structures (i.e. insufficient strength);
- thermal and/or moisture movement of the brickwork (*see* pages 86 and 87);
- thermal and/or moisture movement of associated structures;
- mechanical impact or severe vibration;
- expansive chemical reaction of materials (e.g. sulfate attack of cement mortar);
- corrosion of embedded ferrous metals (e.g. steel joists, lintels and wall ties).

Depending on the severity and extent of cracking there are four repair options available:

- demolition and rebuilding of damaged areas;
- cutting out and replacement of damaged bricks;
- simple surface filling of cracks;
- epoxy resin injection and cosmetic surface filling.

The first three options are traditional repair methods. Because the first is expensive and the third is not generally very effective, except for minor damage, the second option has tended to be the common general repair method. Well-integrated 'invisible' repairs are very difficult to achieve. Nevertheless, with care and skill, repairs can be completed in sympathy with the appearance and character of the original.

Surface filling is relatively simple, and with the use of 'cosmetic' tints can give well-finished results. However, it is superficial and is not effective as a structural repair of a fracture that is still subject to stress. A stronger repair can be made, with little disturbance to the structure, by injecting epoxy resin adhesive to fill and bond the fracture. The bonding material is finished back from the face of the brickwork to allow for cosmetic surface filling to complete the repair. Specialist firms offer appropriate epoxy and polyester resin formulations and an injection service to repair cracks and stabilise areas of distressed brickwork.

Epoxy resin bonding can also be used to secure stainless steel wall ties to replace corroded iron and steel ties in cavity walls. It can also be used to secure anchors and ties to stabilize distressed brickwork.

As an alternative to resin-fixed replacement wall ties, several patterns of proprietary replacement wall ties and stabilizing anchors are manufactured in stainless steel. The designs feature a variety of mechanically expanded materials or mechanisms to grip into sound masonry.

CLEANING BRICKWORK

Some specific forms of staining and their remedial treatment have been described earlier. Dirt and grime generally, particularly that sprayed from roads, can disfigure brickwork and make it look drab and lifeless. It is not necessary for brickwork to be routinely cleaned but, after many years of passive service, some brickwork might benefit from general cleaning to restore its original attractive appearance.

Superficial dirt can be removed by washing with water (hot water may help) using a mild detergent and a soft bristle or nylon brush, followed by rinsing with clean water. Care must be taken not to damage soft bricks, especially carved decorative ones, and bricks with sand-textured surfaces, by harsh scrubbing.

A solution of dishwasher detergent and hot water can be effective on heavier deposits of dirt and grime. Wear rubber gloves for protection. Scrub the surface with the solution using a bristle or nylon brush, leave for about 10 minutes and rinse with clean water. Steam-cleaning equipment is available for hire and can be effective, particularly for soot and smoke stains and greasy or oily deposits.

High-pressure water-jet cleaning can be very effective, but it is abrasive and can damage delicate surface textures and weak materials. Great care is also necessary to avoid scouring mortar from the joints. Before embarking on widespread cleaning with this equipment, experiment on a less important surface first. Try the effectiveness of lower pressure settings first, do not hold the jet very close and keep it moving to prevent too concentrated an impact. Do not proceed if any of the masonry fabric is damaged by the jet. Do not force water into open joints, particularly those at roof verges and eaves and between masonry and window and door frames.

Water cleaning will inevitably wet the masonry and with high-pressure equipment, wetting could be severe. Therefore the work should be undertaken in good drying weather, at a time of year when there is no risk of frost. The excessive wetting may dissolve soluble salts from deep within the brickwork which, as drying out proceeds, causes efflorescence on its surface. Any efflorescence will be temporary and, as described on page 135, can be left to weather away naturally.

Proprietary brick-cleaning solutions available from builders' merchants are usually based on hydrochloric acid and are made to clean mortar and lime staining from new brickwork. They can be used on older brickwork for lime stains, but they are not general cleaners and will not remove other types of stain or general grime.

Gentle cleaning with water and soft bristle brushes can give good results with delicate gauged brickwork and terracotta.

There may be specific disfigurements, e.g. paint, graffiti, oil and tar, that need particular solvents or cleaning agents. The nature of the stain should be identified, so that the appropriate treatment is used otherwise effort and expense will be wasted and inappropriate chemical reactions may result in disfiguring stains.

Recommendations for cleaning a number of common and less common stains that can mar the good appearance of brickwork are available on the Brick Development Association website. Contact details are listed at the end of this book.

Over a long period of time, some forms of grime can form a chemical bond with the siliceous surface

142

Tinting used to match bricks no longer made. The flat roofed extension was built in the red bricks of the band course and quoins, and the grey areas were then tinted to match the grey bricks of the original building.

of clay bricks. This cannot be removed by washing or scrubbing with water and detergents. Specialist cleaners are produced that will remove the surface of clay bricks (and with it the grime). These cleaners are generally based on very powerful acids and often referred to as 'restoration cleaners'. Their manufacturers provide explicit instructions for their use and the safety precautions to be observed when doing so. These must be followed with care because of the very aggressive action of these cleaners and the serious burns they can cause if they come into contact with skin. This work is best left to specialist cleaning contractors with experience in handling such hazardous materials.

Specialist cleaning firms with specific experience in dealing with brickwork will generally be more effective than general building contractors. The work should be done in accordance with BS 8221 Code of Practice for Cleaning and Surface Repair of Buildings – Part 1: *Cleaning of Natural Stones, Brick, Terracotta and Concrete.*

TINTING BRICKWORK

Repairs or extensions to brickwork are sometimes not a very satisfactory match. In Chapter 4, the various factors that affect the appearance of brickwork are noted. If the mismatch is due to colour differences in the bricks or the mortar, then cosmetic tinting can provide a satisfactory correction.

Tinting brickwork by applying colour-fast oxide-based pigments in a potassium silicate medium, to give a permanent tint to the surface of brickwork, has been used with success for about forty years. Experience has shown that such tinting is a permanent modification of surface colour and the treatment has no adverse effects on the durability or other performance attributes of the masonry.

It is mostly used to rectify a mismatch of bricks and/or mortar, or to correct colour banding or a patchy appearance resulting from a failure to blend bricks adequately during bricklaying. But tinting has also been used intentionally in design and specification to create a particular coloration that could not be achieved by the selection of bricks; for example, when new bricks of a particular colour are unobtainable, brickwork can built with bricks of the size and textural character required, and the bricks subsequently tinted to the specific colour. Tinting has also been used to create features of contrasting brick colour in the bond pattern of brickwork after its completion.

Tints must be applied with restraint, as the effect can easily be spoiled if it is too harsh. For this reason, the work should be entrusted to a specialist contractor with appropriate experience and skill. There are only a few specialists offering tinting services in the UK. The Brick Development Association and brick manufacturers will be able to provide contact details for them.

ARTIFICIAL WEATHERING

In many cases, repairs and extensions are a good match, but the newness is too fresh and bright in comparison with their surroundings. Permanent tinting, as described above, should not be used in these instances. If the existing work is very dirty, cleaning it may be the best course of action, but if it is not, the following method of artificial weathering can be used to tone down the new work and blend it in.

The application of soot water is simple, quick and unlikely to create problems for the future. If the bricks are very porous and dry, reduce the suction of the surface by dampening it with clean water prior to treatment. Soak a bag of soot in a container of water until the water is quite dark. Remove the soot bag and, keeping the liquid stirred, apply a wash to the brickwork with a broad brush. Repeat if necessary. A few light applications are preferable to one heavy one. Err on the side of under-treatment. If the desired effect is not achieved when the surface has thoroughly dried off, an additional application can be made. Do not tone the brickwork too much because new bricks will tend to darken naturally in a fairly short time.

Soot, lamp black and other forms of carbon black are traditional pigments no longer available from builders' merchants, but chimney sweeps often supply soot locally for gardening applications.

In rural environments, attractive weathering might include light growths of lichen, moss or similar material. New masonry can be sprayed with a liquid to encourage such growths. A suitable liquid can be made by soaking a bag containing cow pats in a container of warm water overnight. Remove the bag and decant the container to remove large particles. The liquid, which does not have an unpleasant odour, can then be sprayed on dry brickwork. Watered-down yoghurt or milk can also be used. The weathering effect may take some time, but the treatment provides food material to encourage lichen growth.

Glossary

NB   Terms printed in *italics* in the definitions are separately defined within this Glossary.

air entrainer	see '*plasticizer*'
angle grinder	a powered hand tool with a cutting/grinding disc that can be used for cutting bricks or blocks and also for cutting masonry
angles	*special*-shaped bricks, which form non-right angled corners in walls
arch	an assembly of bricks that spans an opening in a wall; it is usually curved in form, but may be flat
arris	any straight edge of a brick formed by the junction of its faces
bat	a part brick, e.g. half-brick, three-quarter-brick, used in *bonding* brickwork at corners and ends of walls
batt	see '*insulation batt*'
batching	the accurate proportioning of *mortar* materials to produce a specified mortar mix
bed	the horizontal layer of mortar on which a brick is laid
bed face	the face(s) of a brick usually laid in contact with a mortar *bed*
bed-joint	an horizontal joint in brickwork
bolster	a broad-bladed chisel of hardened steel used for cutting bricks
bond (1)	the arrangement of bricks in brickwork, usually interlocking, to distribute load
bond (2)	the resistance to displacement of individual bricks in a wall provided by the adhesive function of *mortar*
bonding brick	see '*bat*'
British Standards	standards used in the UK defining the sizes and properties of materials and their proper use in building; these will eventually be withdrawn in favour of *European Standards*
broken bond	the use of part-bricks to modify a *bonding* pattern, where dimensions do not allow a regular bond pattern of full bricks

bullnose	*special*-shaped brick with a curved surface joining two adjacent faces
calcium silicate brick	a brick made from lime and sand (sandlime), possibly with crushed flint (flintlime), processed by steam at high temperature and pressure
capping	construction or component at the top of a wall or parapet not providing a weathered and *throated* overhang (cf. '*coping*')
cavity batten	a timber batten, with lifting wires, sized to temporarily lie in the void of a cavity wall to catch mortar droppings and assist their removal
cavity tray	see '*DPC tray*'
cavity wall	wall of two *leaves* effectively tied together with *wall ties* with a space between them, usually at least 50mm (2in) wide
cement	see '*Portland cement*' and '*masonry cement*'
centring	curved former used to provide temporary support to the underside of an *arch* during its construction
clamp	a large stack of moulded, dried clay bricks and fuel, which is set alight and burns to fire the bricks
clay brick	a brick formed from clay and fired in a *kiln* or *clamp* to produce a hard semi-vitrified unit
closer	*bonding brick* cut to expose a half-*header* in the surface of a wall
club hammer	heavy hammer used with a *bolster* to cut bricks
collar joint	a continuous vertical joint, parallel to the face of a wall, formed in walls one brick or more thick, when bricks are *bonded* in leaves of stretcher bond
common brick	a brick for general purpose use, where appearance is not important
concrete brick	a brick made of crushed rock aggregate bound with *Portland cement*
coping	construction, or component, at the top of a wall or *parapet* that is weathered, *throated* and overhangs the wall surface below to protect it from saturation (cf. '*capping*')
corbel	a feature, or *course*, or courses of brick, projecting from the face of the wall, often forming a support
corner block	a wooden, or plastic, block to provide a temporary fixing at the ends of a wall for a string *line* used to align bricks or blocks when they are laid
course	a row of bricks laid on a mortar *bed* jointed in mortar, generally horizontally
course stuff	a mixture of *sand* and *lime* to which *cement* and water is added to make *mortar*
cross-joint	vertical mortar joint at right angles to the face of the wall (sometimes incorrectly called a '*perp*')
cryptoflorescence	the deposit of crystallized salts within the pores below the surface of brickwork caused by the drying out of a solution of soluble salts washed from the bricks by moisture

datum	a fixed reference point from which levels are set out
damp-proof course (DPC)	a layer or strip of impervious material built into a joint of a wall, chimney or similar construction to prevent the passage of water
DPC brick	*clay brick* of specified maximum *water absorption*, of which two courses may be built at the base of a wall to prevent the upward movement of moisture
DPC tray	a wide *DPC* bedded in the outer leaf, stepping up in the cavity of a *cavity wall*, and built into the inner leaf; it diverts water in the cavity through *weepholes* in the outer leaf
damp-proof membrane (DPM)	a layer or sheet of impervious material within or below a floor, or vertically within or on a wall, to prevent the passage of moisture
durability	the ability of materials to withstand the potentially destructive action of freezing conditions and chemical reactions when in a saturated state
eaves	lower edge of a pitched roof, or edge of a flat roof
efflorescence	a white powdery deposit of crystallized salts on the face of brickwork caused by the drying out of a solution of soluble salts washed from the bricks and/or mortar by excessive wetting
engineering brick	a type of strong, dense clay brick traditionally used for civil engineering work
European Standards	standards used in the European Community defining the sizes and properties of materials and their proper use in building; these will eventually supersede national standards such as British Standards
extruded wire-cut bricks	bricks formed by forcing stiff moist clay, under pressure, through a die and cutting the extruded shape into individual bricks with taught wires
face work	brickwork or blockwork built neatly and evenly without applied finish
facing brick	a brick for use in the exposed surface of brickwork, where consistent and acceptable appearance is required
fireclay	a clay containing a high proportion of silica, principally used for the manufacture of fire bricks because of its resistance to high temperature; also to make building bricks of buff colour
flashing	waterproof flexible sheet material, frequently lead, dressed to prevent entry of rain water at an abutment junction between roof and brickwork
fletton bricks	pressed bricks made from lower Oxford clay, originally in Fletton, near Peterborough, and subsequently extensively used throughout the UK
flintlime brick	see '*calcium silicate brick*'
foundation	a substructure to bear on supporting subsoil; may be piles, ground beams, a raft or concrete strips
frog	an indentation in one or both bed faces of some types of moulded or *pressed bricks*
gable	portion of a wall above eaves level that encloses the end of a pitched roof

gauge rod	batten marked at intervals for vertical setting-out of brick *courses*
gauged arch	an *arch* formed of wedge-shaped bricks jointed with non-tapered mortar joints
gulley	a drainage fitting, usually with a grating, through which water enters a drainage system
handmade bricks	see '*soft-mud bricks*'
hatching and grinning	irregularity of appearance due to the poor vertical alignment of the faces of bricks in a wall surface
hawk	a small board, with a handle in the centre of the underside, used for holding a small quantity of *mortar* ready for *pointing* with a trowel
header	the end face of a standard brick
inspection chamber	chamber (with a cover) to permit access to a drain, sewer or pipe line
insulation batt	rectangular unit of resilient fibrous thermal insulation material of uniform thickness, used to fully fill the air space in a *cavity wall*
insulation board	rectangular unit of rigid thermal insulation material of uniform thickness used to partially fill the air space in a *cavity wall*
insulation material	material primarily intended to resist the passage of heat through a construction
jamb	constructional assembly at the side of a window or door opening
joint profile	the shape of a mortar-joint finish
jointer	a tool used to form a mortar joint *profile*
jointing	forming the finished surface profile of a mortar joint as the work proceeds (cf. '*pointing*')
leaf	one of two parallel walls that are tied together as a *cavity wall*
level (1)	the horizontality of *courses* of brickwork
level (2)	see '*spirit level*'
lime (hydrated)	a fine powdered material, with no appreciable setting and hardening properties, used to improve the workability and water retention of *cement* based *mortars*
lime (hydraulic)	a fine powdered material which, when mixed with water, slowly sets and hardens and binds together to form a solid material; traditionally used as a constituent of *mortar*
lime putty	slaked lime, sieved and mixed with water, possibly with a little fine sand, to form a white *mortar*, traditionally used for thin joints in *gauged arches*
lime stain (bleed or bloom)	white insoluble calcareous deposit on brickwork
line (1)	a string line used to guide the setting of bricks to *line* and *level*
line (2)	the straightness of brickwork

line block	see 'corner block'
lintel	a component of reinforced concrete, steel or timber to support brickwork over an opening
masonry cement	a pre-mixed blend of *Portland cement*, filler material and an *air entrainer* used to mix with *sand* and water to form *mortar*
mortar	a mixture of *sand, cement* or *lime* (or a combination of both) possibly with the inclusion of an *air entrainer*, that hardens after application and is used for jointing brickwork or as *render*
movement joint	a continuous horizontal or vertical joint in brickwork (usually filled with compressible material) to accommodate movement caused by changes in moisture content and temperature
parapet wall	upper part of a wall that bounds a roof, balcony, terrace or bridge
perforated bricks	*extruded wire-cut* bricks with holes through from *bed face* to *bed face*
perpends (perps)	notional vertical lines controlling the verticality of *cross-joints* appearing in the face of a wall
pier	local vertical thickening of a wall to improve its stiffness
pigment	material that may be added to *mortar* to modify its colour
pins	flat-bladed nails temporarily pressed into mortar joints to secure bricklayers *line*
plasticizer	powdered or liquid admixture added to *mortar* in controlled amounts to improve workability by generating air bubbles during mixing; also known as 'air entrainer'
plinth (1)	visible projection or recess at the base of a wall or pier
plinth (2)	*special*-shaped brick chamfered to provide for reduction in thickness between a *plinth* and the rest of a wall
plugging chisel	a chisel with a narrow cutting edge for cutting out hardened *mortar* from joints
plumb	the verticality of brickwork
pointing	finishing a mortar joint by raking out part of the jointing mortar, filling with additional mortar, and tooling or otherwise working it to form a finished *joint profile* (cf. 'pointing')
Portland cement	a fine powdered material that when mixed with water, sets and binds particles together in *mortar* and *concrete*
pressed bricks	bricks formed by pressing moist clay into shape by hydraulic press
profile boards	temporary timber boards erected outside the enclosing walls of a structure at corners and used to fix *string* lines when setting-out *foundations* and walls
quoin	the external corner of a wall
radial brick	*special* curved brick for use in brickwork curved on plan
reference panel	a panel of brickwork built at the commencement of a contract to set standards of appearance and workmanship

render	*mortar* applied to a wall surface as a finish
repointing	the raking out of old *mortar* and replacing it with new (cf. '*pointing*')
retaining wall	a wall that provides support to higher ground at a change of level
returns	the areas of walling at piers or recesses, which are at right angles to the general face of the wall
reveal	the area of walling at the side of an opening, which is at right angles to the general face of the wall
reverse bond	*bonding* in which asymmetry of pattern is accepted across the width of an opening or at *quoins* in order to avoid *broken bond* in the work
rough arch	an *arch* of standard bricks jointed with tapered mortar joints
sandlime brick	see '*calcium silicate brick*'
scale	the proportional relationship between a representation of an object on a construction drawing and its actual size, e.g. ¹⁄₁₀th full size = 1:10 = 1 unit of dimension on a drawing represents 10 in the work
sealant	a stiff fluid material, which sets but does not harden; used to exclude wind driven rain from *movement joints* and around door and window frames
sill (1)	the lower horizontal edge of an opening
sill (2)	bottom horizontal member of a door or window frame, or a separate component used to protect the brickwork below an opening; may be finished flush or project in front of the general plane of the wall
skewback	brickwork, or special-shaped block, which provides an inclined surface from which an *arch* springs
soft-mud bricks	bricks moulded from clay in a moist, mud-like state; often handmade
soldier	a brick laid vertically on end with the *stretcher face* showing in the surface of the work
specials	bricks of special shape or size used for the construction of particular brickwork features
spirit level	device for checking horizontality or verticality consisting of one or more sealed glass tubes, each containing liquid and an air bubble, mounted in a frame
spot board	board on which fresh *mortar* is placed ready for use
springing	plane at the end of an *arch*, which springs from a *skewback*
squint	*special* brick for the construction of non-right angled corners (see also '*angle*')
stock bricks	*soft-mud bricks*, traditionally handmade, but now often machine moulded
stop end	a three-sided box-shaped shoe of *DPC* material sealed to the end of a *DPC* tray to divert the discharge of water
storey rod	*gauge rod* of storey height with additional marks to indicate features such as *lintel* bearings, *sills*, floor joists

stretcher	the longer face of a brick showing in the surface of a wall
stud	a vertical member of a timber-framed wall structure
sulfate attack	a chemical reaction of soluble sulfates from the ground, or certain bricks, with a constituent of *Portland cement* that can damage *mortar*
throated (coping or sill)	with a groove (drip) formed on the underside of and parallel to the edge of a coping or projecting sill to prevent water running back onto the surface of the walling below
tie	a fixing, generally metal, to connect and/or stabilize brickwork, e.g. cladding to a backing; see also '*wall tie*'
tingle plate	a plate shaped to give intermediate support to a *line*
trammel	timber batten, pivoted at one end, used to set out curved work
trowel	hand tool with a thin, flat, kite-shaped blade for applying mortar
tuck pointing	a type of *pointing* in which the mortar is finished flush with the wall surface and tinted to match the bricks; then fine strips of *lime putty* are pressed onto the surface of the work to simulate fine, precisely placed, *bed-* and *cross-joints* (in the USA the term means ordinary *pointing*)
U-value	a measurement of heat flow through a building element, e.g. a wall, roof or floor, used to compare thermal insulation performance of various assemblies; the unit of measurement is w/m^2k
voussior	a wedge-shaped brick or stone used in a *gauged arch*
verge	sloping edge of a pitched roof
wall tie	a component, made of metal or plastic, built into the two leaves of a *cavity wall* to link them together (see also '*tie*')
water absorption	a measure of the density of a brick by calculating the percentage increase in the weight of a saturated brick compared with its dry weight
weephole	a hole through brickwork, usually an unmortared *cross-joint*, through which water can drain to its outer face

Further Reading

Brick Development Association, *Design Note:*
DN 8: *Rigid Paving with Clay Pavers*
DN 9: *Flexible Paving with Clay Pavers*
DN 12: *The Design of Curved Brickwork*
DN 13: *The Use of Bricks of Special Shape*
DN 15: *Brick Cladding to Timber Frame Construction*

These publications provide detailed information and recommendations on particular aspects of brick-work design and detail. They are not intended as craft training textbooks. Available from BDA (*see* Useful Contacts).

Brick Development Association, *The BDA Guide to Successful Brickwork* (2nd edn) (Butterworth Heinemann, 2000)
ISBN 0 3407589906

This book is especially recommended for its copious illustrations and detailed description of brickwork construction. It is intended for vocational craft training, but it starts from simple basic work and majority of detail concerns domestic building construction.

Brunskill, R.W., *Brick Building in Britain* (Victor Gollancz/Peter Crawley, 1990) ISBN 0 575 06535 4

Recommended as an authoritative account of the history of brickmaking and brick building in Britain from the fourteenth to the late-twentieth century. The highly readable text is well illustrated.

Building Research Establishment, *Good Building Guides:*
GBG 14: Building Simple Plain Brick or Blockwork Freestanding Walls
GBG 19: Building Reinforced, Diaphragm and Wide Plan Freestanding Walls
GBG 27: Building Brick or Blockwork Retaining Walls

These publications provide details of safe designs for walls suitable for domestic applications in various parts of the British Isles. Available from BRE (*see* Useful Contacts).

Hodge, J.C., revised Baldwin, R., *Brickwork for Apprentices* (4th edn) (Butterworth Heinemann, 1993) ISBN 0 340 55641 2

This craft training textbook deals extensively with bonding details for various configurations of walling, decorative brickwork, arches and other advanced work.

Knight, T. *Creative Brickwork* (Butterworth Heinemann, 1997) ISBN 0 340 67643 4

A guide for architects and building supervisors illustrating the more decorative applications of brickwork in modern commercial and public buildings.

Useful Contacts

BRICK MANUFACTURERS' TRADE ASSOCIATIONS

The following trade associations represent manufacturers of clay bricks and pavers in their respective countries and can give contact details of member companies. They produce a range of publications that give guidance on the application of bricks and pavers, and their websites have technical information that can be downloaded free of charge. The websites also provide links to members and related organizations.

United Kingdom and Ireland
Brick Development Association
Woodside House, Winkfield, Windsor, Berkshire SL4 2DX
Tel: 01433 885651 www.brick.org.uk

United States of America
Brick Industry Association
11490 Commerce Park Drive, Reston, VA 20191-1525, USA
Tel: 703.620.0010 www.bia.org
Brick Association of the Carolinas
Suite 800, 8420 University Executive Park Drive, Charlotte, North Carolina 28262, USA
Tel: 704.510.1500 www.gobrick.com
Southern Brick Institute
1810 Overlake Drive-Suite A, Conyers, GA 30013, USA
Tel: 770.760.0728 www.gobrick.com

Australia
Clay Brick and Paver Institute
PO Box 6567, Baulkham Hills BC, New South Wales 2153, Australia
Tel: (02) 9629 4922 www.claybrick.com.au

BRICK MANUFACTURERS

Many manufacturers provide helpful information on the application of their products. Contact details are too numerous to list here. The trade associations noted above will provide contact details of their members, including live links on their websites.

MORTAR

Mortar Industry Association
156 Buckingham Palace Road, London SW1W 9TR
Tel: 020 7730 8194 www.mortar.org.uk

Gives information and advice on mortars for brick and block masonry and rendering. Downloadable specification information is available on the website, also contact details for suppliers of ready-mixed mortar.

Natural Lime Mortars

Bursledon Brickworks (Trading) Ltd
Coal Park Lane, Swanwick, Southampton, Hampshire SO31 7GW
Tel: 01489 576248

Supplier of traditional building materials including hydraulic lime, lime putty, ochre and pigments and a variety of ready-mixed lime mortars for brickwork and rendering. Advice on the use of traditional materials is available also a mortar analysis and mortar matching service.

Hydraulic Lias Limes Ltd
Melmoth House, Abbey Close, Sherborne, Dorset DT9 3LH
Tel: 01935 817220 www.limesolve.demon.co.uk

Producer of natural hydraulic lime for brickwork and rendering mortars. This company has a British Board of Agrément (BBA) Certificate approving the use of mortar made with its lime in certain types of building and following specified procedures.

NB: Specifiers intent on using lime-bound mortars in new building should understand that such a use is beyond the scope of current British Standard codes of practice for masonry design and specification (2001). Therefore they should satisfy themselves that the technical guidance upon which they depend is suitably authoritative. Also that the use of lime-bound mortar will not limit any insurance being sought for the new building under a warranty scheme such as that operated by the National House Building Council.

TECHNICAL GUIDANCE

Building Research Establishment
Garston, Watford, Hertfordshire WD2 7JR
Tel: 01923 664000. For publications: www.brebookshop.com

This organization provides an information service and publishes a large number of publications. The *BRE Good Building Guide* and *BRE Digest* series contain several titles relevant to brickwork masonry.

British Cement Association
Telford House, Crowthorne, Berkshire RG11 6YS
Tel: 01344 762676

This is the trade association for cement and concrete products. Several publications are available including guidance on foundations and rendering.

BUILDERS' MERCHANTS

Builders' Merchants Federation
15 Soho Square, London W1D 3HL
Tel. 0870 901 3380 www.bmf.org.uk

Provides addresses of builders merchant members of the Federation. Also listed on website.

RECLAIMED BRICKS

SALVO
PO Box 333, Cornhill-on-Tweed, Northumberland TD12 4YJ
Website: www.salvo.co.uk

Provides addresses of specialist dealers listed by county.

SELF-BUILD MAGAZINE

Build It
Inside Communications Ltd, The Isis Building, Thames Quay, 193 Marsh Wall, London E14 9SG
Tel: 020 7772 8300 www.buildit-online.co.uk

Monthly magazine dealing with self-build houses, conversions and renovations. Informative website. Land finding service.

Index